TRAINING
for
RACIAL EQUITY
and
INCLUSION:

A GUIDE TO SELECTED PROGRAMS

D1319030

Written by

Ilana Shapiro, Ph.D.

TO ORDER:

Additional copies of
*Training for Racial Equity & Inclusion:
A Guide to Selected Programs*
can be obtained from:
The Aspen Institute
Fullfillment Office
P.O. Box 222
109 Houghton Lab Lane
Queenstown, Maryland 21658
Phone: (410) 820-5338
Fax: (410) 827-9174
E-mail: publications@aspeninstitute.org

The Aspen Institute
One Dupont Circle, NW
Washington, DC 20036-1133
Published in the United States of America
in 2002 by The Aspen Institute

PRODUCED BY:

The Project Change Anti-Racism Initiative: Project Change was established in 1991 as an initiative of Levi Strauss & Company through its corporate foundation. The project addresses racial prejudice and institutional racism in four communities throughout the United States: Albuquerque, New Mexico; El Paso, Texas; Knoxville, Tennessee; and Valdosta, Georgia. Project Change unites community leaders serving diverse constituencies and assists them in developing leadership capacities that both complement and transcend their racial and ethnic interests.

Shirley Strong, Executive Director

The Aspen Institute Roundtable on Comprehensive Community Initiatives for Children and Families: The Aspen Institute Roundtable is a forum for leaders working to improve the life circumstances of children and families in distressed urban neighborhoods. It provides a venue where they can discuss challenges, emerging lessons and work on issues of common concern. The Roundtable also serves as a clearinghouse for information about community change efforts and undertakes in-depth work on key dilemmas facing the field. This publication is one product of a longer-term project examining structural racism and community revitalization, funded by the Annie E. Casey Foundation, the Charles S. Mott Foundation and the Robert Wood Johnson Foundation.

Anne Kubisch and Karen Fulbright-Anderson, Co-Directors

IN CONSULTATION WITH:

Center for Assessment and Policy Development: The Center for Assessment and Policy Development (CAPD) is a non-profit research, planning and policy organization based outside Philadelphia. Founded in 1988, its mission is to improve the quality of life for children, adolescents, families and neighborhoods by helping to build the capacity of organizations, collaborations, government, schools and others who do the day-to-day work on their behalf. Through their evaluation, CAPD helps people use the tools of democracy—leadership, civic engagement, anti-racism work, system reform, public will, outcome tracking—to build stronger communities, particularly for children, adolescents and families.

Sally Leiderman, President

WRITTEN BY:

Ilana Shapiro has a doctorate in Social Psychology and is completing a second doctorate in Conflict Analysis and Resolution at George Mason University. She is the President of the Alliance for Conflict Transformation (ACT), a non-profit organization dedicated to expanding the knowledge and practice of conflict transformation in U.S. and international communities. Her work focuses on integrating theory, research and practice to develop appropriate interventions into racial and ethnic conflicts in the U.S., Middle East and Central and Eastern Europe.

PROJECT HISTORY

IN 1992, FACED WITH THE daunting task of choosing a training program to assist in developing its anti-racism initiatives, Project Change commissioned Gary Delgado and the Applied Research Center to conduct a study of ten programs. The goal was to better understand the differences among these ten anti-racism programs, assess their potential utility in assisting community organizations like Project Change, and address some of the critical issues around anti-racism activities and programs. The resulting publication, *Anti-Racist Work: An Examination and Assessment of Organizational Activity* made a crucial contribution to the field by advancing a structural analysis of racism and assessing organizational activities through that lens. It also pioneered an important conceptual and research framework for understanding and differentiating anti-racism organizations and activities.

Ten years later, recognizing the changing nature of race relations in U.S. communities and the variety of new training programs that had emerged to address racial and ethnic prejudice, oppression and diversity, Project Change commissioned this *Guide* to build upon and update the 1992 publication. Project Change selected the Center for Assessment and Policy Development (CAPD) to draw upon their considerable experience and expertise in program assessment in leading this initiative. CAPD, in turn, designated Ilana Shapiro, President of the Alliance for Conflict Transformation, as the principal researcher because this project closely paralleled her own research—a comparative analysis of interventions addressing racial and ethnic tensions in U.S. communities.

A natural partnership with the Aspen Institute Roundtable on Comprehensive Community Initiatives for Children and Families soon formed, based on a shared focus on the importance of addressing structural racism and a common interest in developing racial justice "tools" for community leaders and organizations. The Aspen Roundtable's team has been an integral part of supporting, designing, collecting and analyzing data, editing and publishing this study.

Together, Project Change in Oakland, California, the Aspen Institute Roundtable on Comprehensive Communities Initiatives for Children and Families in New York City, the Center for Assessment and Policy Development in Philadelphia, Pennsylvania, and the Alliance for Conflict Transformation in Fairfax, Virginia formed a cooperative partnership to develop this publication.

ACKNOWLEDGEMENTS

WHILE I HAVE TAKEN THE lead in collecting information and writing this publication, this study was truly a cooperative effort. As such, there are numerous people to thank.

First, many thanks go to the directors, trainers and staff of all the programs reviewed in this study who expressed excitement and support for this project. They trusted us with their materials, gave us access to their trainings, and provided reflective, candid interviews. I extend sincere appreciation to the directors and trainers of these excellent programs for their significant contributions to this *Guide* through interviews and comments on their program summaries including: **Sharon Martinas** and **Chris Crass** at Challenging White Supremacy Workshop; **Tema Okun** at Change*work;* **Joe Barndt** and **Chuck Ruehle** at Crossroads Ministry; **Patricia Harbour** at Healing the Heart of Diversity; **Rob Corcoran** at Hope in the Cities; **Larry Bell** at National Coalition Building Institute, Washington, D.C.; **Reggie Williams** and **Martin Rafanan** at the National Conference for Community and Justice, St. Louis, MO; **John Maguire** at the National Network for Anti-Racism and Community Building Institutes; **Ron Chisom** and **Barbara Majors** at the People's Institute for Survival and Beyond; **Emily Style** and **Peggy McIntosh** at Seeking Educational Equity and Diversity; **John Landesman** at Study Circles Resource Center; **Antje Mattheus** and **George Lakey** at Training for Change; **Valerie Batts** at Vigorous InterventionS Into Ongoing Natural Settings; and **Lindsay Friedman** at the Anti-Defamation League. I am additionally grateful to **Lindsay Friedman** for her helpful suggestions about questions for selecting a training program and to **Maggie Potapchuk,** at the Joint Center for Political and Economic Studies, for her insightful comments on several program summaries.

This *Guide* would not be possible without the intensive collaboration of the project team. **Shirley Strong,** Executive Director of Project Change, had the vision, leadership, insight and unfaltering commitment to furthering the field that inspired and organized this project. **Sally Leiderman,** President of CAPD, brought indispensable guidance and sage judgment to bear throughout the research and writing process. **Anne Kubisch,** Co-Director of the Aspen Institute Roundtable, inspired all of us with her wisdom, encouragement, generous spirit of collaboration and practical leadership in bringing this project to completion. **Khatib Waheed,** Senior Program Associate, at the Aspen Institute Roundtable, shared his profound understanding of the issues and was an invaluable partner in collecting data and discussing pressing concerns in this field. **Karen Fulbright-Anderson,** Co-Director, and **Keith Lawrence,** Senior Program Associate at the Aspen Institute Roundtable, contributed excellent ideas and suggestions that were essential in shaping this *Guide.*

I am incredibly grateful to **Gretchen Susi** at the Aspen Institute Roundtable and **Leila Feister** for their crucial and masterful work in editing and strengthening the final document.

Finally, I am abidingly grateful to Robert Harris, my husband, for his untiring love and support throughout this project, and for his thoughtful comments and reflections on multiple drafts of this *Guide.* I dedicate this guide to my son, Benjamin Micah. He was born in the midst of this research and his life and spirit have inspired me in untold ways over the past seven months. May the many efforts to build racial equity and inclusion help create a new and more hopeful legacy for this next generation.

I hope the *Guide* has done justice to the programs it reviewed, that it will spark new thoughts and discussion in the field, and most of all that it will be useful to those who read through it.

–Ilana Shapiro, Ph.D.
April, 2002

TABLE *of* CONTENTS

PROJECT HISTORY IV

OVERVIEW 1

Section One   Program Summaries

1. PEOPLE'S INSTITUTE FOR SURVIVAL AND BEYOND 7

2. NATIONAL COALITION BUILDING INSTITUTE 15

3. VISIONS—VIGOROUS INTERVENTIONS INTO ONGOING NATURAL SETTINGS 23

4. WORLD OF DIFFERENCE® INSTITUTE—ANTI-DEFAMATION LEAGUE 31

5. CROSSROADS MINISTRY 39

6. STUDY CIRCLES RESOURCE CENTER 47

7. HOPE IN THE CITIES 55

8. DISMANTLING RACISM INSTITUTE—NATIONAL CONFERENCE FOR COMMUNITY AND JUSTICE 63

9. CHALLENGING WHITE SUPREMACY WORKSHOP 71

10. WHITE PEOPLE WORKING ON RACISM, TRAINING FOR CHANGE 79

Section Two   Important Related Work

*Seed-Seeking Educational Equity and Diversity 89, Changework 91,
Healing the Heart of Diversity 93, National Network of Anti-Racism and
Community Buildings Institutes 95*

Section Three   Similarities and Differences Across Programs 99

Section Four   Challenges and Implications 109

QUESTIONS GUIDING THE SELECTION OF A TRAINING PROGRAM 113

APPENDICES 115

BIBLIOGRAPHY 123

WHEN WE TALK ABOUT RACE, we don't mean a biological or genetic category, but rather, a way of interpreting differences between people which creates or reinforces inequalities among them. In other words, "race" is an unequal relationship between social groups, represented by the privileged access to power and resources by one group over another.

Race is socially constructed, created (and recreated) by how people are perceived and treated in the normal actions of everyday life. As such, "race" is never fixed. It is a dynamic, constantly changing relationship. Some groups which are defined as an "inferior race" within American society at a certain historical moment may successfully escape racialization and become part of the privileged majority, the "whites." Other groups, especially those who are descended from African, Latino, American Indian, Pacific Islander, and Asian descent, have found the path for group socioeconomic mobility far more difficult.

The unequal boundaries of color have been at times permanent barriers to the economic development, educational and social advancement for millions of Americans, living in what for them was a deeply flawed and often hypocritical democracy.

MANNING MARABLE

Structural Racism and American Democracy
September, 2000

During the 1990s, the growing diversity of American communities invigorated public discourse about racial and ethnic prejudice, intolerance, oppression and conflict. In response, non-profit organizations across the United States developed innovative training programs to address racism and the changing shape of race relations. Although every intervention approaches racial issues and solutions differently, collectively these programs offer many successful examples of transforming people's attitudes and behaviors, intergroup relationships, and social institutions and policies. Yet few efforts have been made to recognize and compare the variety of programs' philosophies, methods and intended outcomes—a process that would help practitioners, community leaders, policy makers and funders identify good practices and develop better models.

Training for Racial Equity and Inclusion: A Guide to Selected Programs aims to fill that gap by providing an in-depth review and comparison of 10 training programs. It describes why programs do what they do (theory of practice) and how they believe their approaches will produce positive results (theory of change).[1] Specifically, it examines how programs understand the sources and dynamics of racial and ethnic oppression and what principles and methods they use to address the problems. In addition, it assesses organizational capacities and the connection between programs' activities and intended outcomes.[2]

The *Guide* is intended to help community leaders, organizations, policy makers, funders

Focus of This Guide

- What are programs' underlying theories of practice and change?
- What training methods do they use and why?
- What are programs' goals and intended outcomes?
- What are programs' services and capacities?

and other stakeholders select and support approaches that best suit their needs and goals. It therefore highlights many types of training, recognizing that no single solution exists to the complex, deep-rooted problems of racial and ethnic oppression. Each program reviewed here offers a unique and compelling approach that will likely appeal to a specific audience.

The *Guide* also encourages people who use these training services to expand their understanding of issues by experiencing more than one program, and to view their participation as the first step in an enduring commitment to racial equity and inclusion.

Selection of Programs

The 10 training programs reviewed in this *Guide* were selected systematically but not scientifically. A survey of professionals knowledgeable about racial issues and programs, and a review of relevant program guides generated an initial list of programs. The project's team members reviewed this list using their own knowledge as researchers and

---

1. *Theory of practice* refers to assumptions about the causes or sources of a problem that guide the choice of strategies and actions to address it. *Theory of change* refers to the process through which change occurs as a result of strategies and actions.

2. See appendices for the interview questions and observation protocol used in the study.

practitioners and their familiarity with key organizations. All programs finally chosen for the study were:

- Grounded in a conceptual analysis of racial and ethnic oppression and social change

- Based in non-profit, non-governmental organizations that work with community groups and leaders from all over the U.S.

- Providers of discrete training sessions as well as long-term consulting, coaching, or technical assistance relationships

- Well-known by professionals knowledgeable about race-related programs

- Well-reviewed by participants and/or identified as "promising programs" in other publications

In addition, we placed a priority on programs that address the institutional and structural dimensions of racism. Many training programs focus on individual and intergroup dynamics of oppression and draw from psychological and cultural research. Fewer programs are grounded in a sociological and political analysis of structural racism, a critically important issue in the post-civil-rights era. We focused on programs that examine the underlying conditions that foster racial disparity and division in U.S. communities. We believe that racial reconciliation and healing must be built on a strong foundation of social and economic justice.

Data Collection

The information presented in the *Guide* comes from: telephone and in-person interviews with program directors, trainers and participants; participant observations of at least one training per organization (for programs in Section One); and a review of training and program materials. We conducted interviews and observations between March 2001 and February 2002. All program directors had an opportunity to review their summaries to ensure that we presented their information accurately.

Using the Guide

The *Guide* is primarily descriptive and analytical. Neither the individual summaries nor the comparative analysis in this *Guide* evaluate the programs or judge their relative effectiveness. Each summary in Section One paints a portrait of a program. Collectively the summaries inform us about the diverse meaning of exemplary practice, and the struggles programs face in transforming individuals, group dynamics and social structures. Section Two outlines four additional programs that we recognized as conducting important related work. Section Three briefly sketches the broader landscape of the field by highlighting some of the similarities and differences across programs. Section Four identifies some major themes, challenges and implications for further work.

Finally, a word about words. We encouraged the people we interviewed to use their own language to describe their work, but the variety of definitions they used posed a challenge when it came time to describe the work across programs. The *Guide*'s use of terms such as 'addressing racial and ethnic oppression' or 'building racial equity and inclusion' are compromises that may not fully capture the subtle distinctions between programs or reconcile the tensions between approaches.

Our effort to find an acceptable shared language reflects a larger struggle to recognize the common ground that these programs share. By highlighting the variety of innovative approaches that exist, this *Guide* seeks to advance cooperation and coordination among programs and strengthen all efforts to build racial equity and inclusion in U.S. communities.

People's Institute for Survival and Beyond • National Coalition Building Institute • VISIONS—Vigorous InterventionS into Ongoing Natural Settings • World of Difference® Institute—Anti-Defamation League • Crossroads Ministry • Study Circles Resource Center • Hope in the Cities • Dismantling Racism Institute—National Conference for Community and Justice • Challenging White Supremacy Workshop • White People Working on Racism—Training for Change • People's

PROGRAM SUMMARIES

THE SUMMARIES FORMAT

THE TEN PROGRAMS IN THIS section are presented chronologically by their date of establishment from the earliest to the most recent. The format of these summaries is briefly described here to orient readers.

Each program begins with a *Summary Chart* that outlines the key elements discussed later in the text. The chart sections include:

Organizational Focus—The key terms used by the program to identify the problem and the solution addressed in their trainings

Organizational History and Context—Date of establishment; history of program development; theories and contexts in which the program is rooted; mission statement

Theory of Practice—Where organization fits into the categories of theories of practice described further in Section Three

Organizational Capacity—Number of offices and trainers; materials available

Services—Types of services and trainings offered

Types of Participants—Primary audiences for services

Level of Analysis—Whether the program works primarily with individual, intergroup relations, or institutional and systemic analysis

Problem Analysis—How the programs explain the problem they focus on and its causes

Intervention Principles—Principles for addressing the problem that help guide the design and strategies of the training

Training Methods—Length of training; primary training methods; structure of the training

Intended Outcomes—The Program's goals and expected outcomes

Theory of Change—Implicit understanding of how program strategies and actions will bring about the desired changes or outcomes

Contact Information—Program director, address, phone/fax, e-mail, and/or website

A textbox entitled *Setting the Scene* provides a snapshot of an exercise and atmosphere typical to that training program. These snapshots are often composite pictures based on researchers' observations of one or more trainings, and are designed to highlight a unique feature of the program. Unless otherwise noted, all quotes in the summaries are taken from program materials or interviews with program staff.

The text summarizing each program is divided into four sections including: *1) Organizational Context; 2) Understanding and Intervening in the Problem; 3) Theory of Change; and 4) Distinguishing Features.* The general features of each section are explained below.

Organizational Context provides an overview of organizational information and is subdivided into three sections. *Mission and History* reviews the program's mission, its development over time, and the theoretical traditions in which its practices are rooted. *Organizational Capacity* describes the size of the program, identifies types of trainings offered, and provides information about program trainers and trainer development. Finally, *Types of Participants* examines the kinds of participants that the programs are designed for, including the levels of leadership, and whether the program typically works with multi-racial or separate race-based groups. All of these elements effect the programs' capacity, credibility and sustainability, and indirectly influence the shape and development of each program's theory of practice and change. This influence is explored further in Section Three of the *Guide.*

The *Understanding and Intervening in the Problem* section focuses on programs' theory of practice and is also divided into three sections. *Understanding the Problem* identifies how each program sets the boundaries of and focuses attention on problems such as prejudice, intolerance, racism, etc., and suggests a coherent explanation that allows them to say what is wrong and in what direction the situation needs to be changed. It focuses on the way programs name and frame the problem that they then try to address through their trainings. *Addressing the Problem*, looks at how programs frame their intervention or advocate what is needed to effectively address the problem they have identified. This analysis provides an overview of the primary principles that guide the training design and discusses how a program's activities contributes to solving the identified problem. *Training Methods* briefly reviews the training design including primary training tools and techniques and training manuals and materials available to participants. It also examines the general structure and flow of trainings, including the main topic areas, exercises and issues addressed.

The *Theory of Change* section briefly looks at the program's implicit understandings of how change happens and how their specific strategies and methods foster individual, intergroup and/or structural change. It also identifies some of the program's intended or expected outcomes.

The *Distinguishing Features* section highlights those features that are unique strengths of the programs. It also includes assessments provided directly by trainers, informal comments by participants, outside reviews of the program, and the researcher's assessments.

Finally, the *Theory of Practice and Change Flowchart* included at the end of each summary provides a visual overview of the relationship between the programs' problem analysis, intervention framing and goals, methods, theory of change, and intended outcomes that are described in the text. It is designed to illustrate the web of understandings shaping the program's underlying theory of practice and change.

These short program summaries cannot adequately capture the richness and depth of each program's efforts and activities. However, they will hopefully provide potential clients, partners and funders with some initial information that encourages them to learn more about those programs that best fit their needs and goals.

1

People's Institute for Survival and Beyond

> *"If racism was constructed,*
>
> *it can be undone.*
>
> *It can be undone*
>
> *if people understand*
>
> *when it was constructed,*
>
> *why it was constructed,*
>
> *how it functions,*
>
> *and how it is maintained."*

PEOPLE'S INSTITUTE FOR SURVIVAL AND BEYOND

SUMMARY INFORMATION

ORGANIZATIONAL FOCUS	**Problem:** Structural racism, white privilege, internalized oppression, institutional gatekeepers. **Solution:** Analysis of racism, social change, justice and equity, self-determination, accountable leadership, community organizing.
ORGANIZATIONAL HISTORY & CONTEXT	Founded in 1980 by Ron Chisom and Jim Dunn. Rooted in community organizing and activism. Mission: "…to build a multi-cultural, anti-racist movement for social change."
THEORY OF PRACTICE	Anti-Racism.
ORGANIZATIONAL CAPACITY	Four regional offices. Ten senior trainers and thirty resource trainers. Publication on program's analysis of racism.
SERVICES	Two-day Undoing Racism training. Assessments, consulting and advanced training for community organizations when requested.
TYPES OF PARTICIPANTS	Primarily community leaders and activists. Community organizations, social service agencies, tenant welfare rights organizations, environmental groups, health groups, city planners, schools, parent groups, youth groups, women's groups, etc.
LEVEL OF ANALYSIS	Structural.
PROBLEM ANALYSIS	Institutional and systemic racism stem from historic systems of racial privilege and oppression, lack of self-determination in communities of color, institutional gatekeeping, internalized racial oppression and dehumanization and lack of a uniting analytical framework.
INTERVENTION PRINCIPLES	Creating a multi-cultural, anti-racism movement requires working from a common set of definitions and an analytical framework for understanding the dynamics of structural racism that empowers communities and serves as the basis for organizing.
TRAINING METHODS	Standard training model rooted in communities of color. Presentation and large group discussion as primary learning tools.
INTENDED OUTCOMES	New understandings of structural racism. Accountable anti-racism leadership. Whites speaking out against structural racism. Self-determination in communities of color. Institutional and systemic change toward equity and justice.
THEORY OF CHANGE	Challenge and motivate people to change. Provide a common analytical frame work for community organizing. Develop new, accountable leadership.
CONTACT INFORMATION	Director: Ron Chisom 1444 North Johnson Street, New Orleans, LA 70116 phone: 504-944-2354

Mission & History

The People's Institute for Survival and Beyond (People's Institute) was established in 1980 by Ron Chisom and Jim Dunn with a mission to "...build a multi-cultural, anti-racist movement for social change." The People's Institute training model provides a common language, set of definitions and analytical framework to talk about and work against institutional and systemic racism in the U.S. Over two decades of experience organizing against racism in communities of color have helped shaped the program's Undoing Racism training model and its assessment, consulting and advanced training services for community leaders.

The program's training model is rooted in community organizing efforts of the 1960s and 1970s that encouraged citizen activists to reclaim their role in and rights to self-determination. These models provided skills and tools for community action against injustice, but because they were designed and conducted primarily by white leaders, often did not take into account the significance of race, culture and history. The People's Institute has developed an analysis that grounds community organizing and social justice efforts in cultural contexts and a focus on structural racism.

Organizational Capacity

The People's Institute has four regional offices, including its headquarters in New Orleans, and additional offices in Berkeley, CA, Brooklyn, NY, and Seattle, WA. Over the past twenty years, the People's Institute has trained more than 35,000 people through their primary activity—a two-day Undoing Racism training model. The program has ten senior trainers and an additional 30 specialized trainers or trainers-in-training who represent a variety of racial, ethnic and cultural groups. The model explicitly focuses on racism

---

SETTING THE SCENE

IN A LARGE room of a community center in the heart of an African American neighborhood of New Orleans, 32 people have gathered for a two-day Undoing Racism training. This regional training, one of four that the New Orleans headquarters of the People's Institute for Survival and Beyond offers each year, has attracted a multi-racial group of participants from social service agencies and community organizations across the east coast of the U.S. Two trainers now stand at the front of the room quickly sketching a picture of the buildings and streets of an urban neighborhood on flipchart paper.

"What are the physical landmarks of poor neighborhoods in this country?" asks one of the trainers. Slowly the participants begin to call out answers: "out of business signs," "cement playgrounds," "liquor stores."

The trainers quickly draw these suggestions into the picture with colorful markers..."cop cars,"

"pawnshops," "churches," "housing projects," "billboards for cigarettes and liquor," "people of color."

The trainers pause for a moment and consider the brightly colored picture before them. Then they draw a big red circle around the picture and ask, "What institutions or systems have an impact on this neighborhood and the people who live here?" Outside the red circle they write up participants' answers: "education," "health care," "criminal justice system."

In an engaging voice, one of the trainers begins describing some of the connections between institutional policies and this neighborhood. Soon all of the participants are involved in an animated discussion about the relationship between race, poverty and institutional practices and policies, and the picture is quickly filled with a web of colorful lines connecting the institutions and the neighborhood. Over the next couple of days participants continue to explore this analysis of systemic racism that will help inform their future community activism and organizing efforts.

within the U.S., but the People's Institute has adapted it to conduct trainings in Japan, Puerto Rico and other locations around the world.

The program's training model emerged primarily out of activist work in African American communities and initially focused on black-white dynamics of racism. Both the model's focus and the organization's trainers have expanded to include many other people of color. The analytical framework remains binary with a focus on the dynamics between whites and people of color, rather than relations among people of color, and is still strongly influenced by its roots in African American communities and cultures.

The People's Institute's work has inspired the development of at least three other organizations that use a similar analytical framework of racism, but have developed unique methods and work with different populations. For example, Challenging White Supremacy Workshop in San Francisco, CA works almost exclusively with young, white community activists and organizers; Crossroads Ministry in Chicago, IL works with a variety of religious, educational and other institutions (see program summaries in this section); and Change*work* in North Carolina works with non-profit organizations and corporations (see Section Three). These programs occasionally cooperate and share materials with each other.

Types of Participants

The People's Institute offers trainings to a broad range of participants including community organizations, social service agencies, tenant welfare rights organizations, environmental groups, health groups, city planners, schools, parent groups, youth groups, women's groups, organizers, activists and leaders, as well as institutional gatekeepers—people in roles that determine access to institutional services. The trainings usually involve multi-racial groups, but the program also offers trainings exclusively for particular communities of color. The program

rarely works with all-white groups or with corporations because of their resistance to the model's analysis of racism.

UNDERSTANDING & INTERVENING AGAINST RACISM

Understanding the Problem

The People's Institute has a strong sociological, historical, and community organizing approach to understanding and addressing racism. The training model suggests that the problem of racism takes several forms, including: the normative behavior of individuals, the policies of institutions, the invasion of a dominant culture, the medium of language, and the military targeting and enforcement of oppressive policies against people of color.

The People's Institute asserts that modern racism is embedded in historic systems of oppression that sustain white wealth, power and privilege. The cumulative effects of institutional, cultural, linguistic, military and normative oppression of communities of color over time have been the widespread disempowerment, disorganization and perpetuation of poverty within these communities. The program's analysis suggests that racism and poverty are intricately linked because people of color do not have control over the institutions and policies that directly impact their lives.

The model suggests that when people learn that they are invisible and worthless, they treat themselves and others like them that way. Internalized oppression has resulted in serious social problems within and between communities of color such as violence, crime, drug addictions, health problems and political apathy. These dynamics also result in the separation and isolation of people of color by class, color and physical location.

The processes of internalized racial inferiority are mirrored in the interlocking dynamic of racial superiority. For many whites, the internalization of superiority renders the systems of power, privilege and preferential treatment invisible. Reinforced by unexamined systems of individualism, competition and capitalism, a cycle of blaming the victim can be an inherent part of internalized superiority and inferiority.

The model particularly focuses on the role of institutional gatekeepers—or those who speak for, describe, translate, interpret, count and determine institutional access for people of color—in the process of systemic oppression. Gatekeepers are typically accountable to their bosses in institutions rather than the communities that they serve, and usually help maintain rather than change the system. They contribute to depriving oppressed people access to the institutions that control their lives.

Finally, the program suggests that not having a common set of definitions and analytical framework for understanding racism is one of the primary obstacles to unified, anti-racist action. The unclear, fragmented and competing discourses about racism and lack of critical power analysis serve to divide people of color, poor whites and anti-racist activists, and prevent united social movements for equity and justice. The People's Institute focuses on racism as the defining form of oppression in the U.S. that serves to maintain all other forms of oppression and acts as the most critical barrier to effective community organizing for social change.[3]

Addressing the Problem

The People's Institute training model suggests that the best way to address these problems is to develop a clear understanding of them. This includes using a common analytical framework and set of definitions as the basis for community organizing. The model recognizes that community organizing and undoing racism are

> "...effective community change cannot happen unless those who would make change understand how race and racism function as a barrier to community, self determination and self sufficiency."

inseparable and suggest that the technical or mechanical skills of organizing are simply not enough for developing a successful liberation movement. Community organizing efforts must be rooted in a common, critical analysis of structural racism in the U.S.

The training model provides education about disempowerment and systemic oppression, accountable leadership in communities and institutions, and organizing across racial lines for social transformation and self-determination. The program emphasizes humanistic values and recognizes the importance of bringing personal experience to understanding racism in order to counteract its dehumanizing effects. However, trainings remain focused on a structural analysis of racism rather than on emotional responses or the personal journey of anti-racism work. The model challenges all participants to be responsible, accountable and active in changing systems of oppression, yet avoids blaming individuals for consciously establishing or perpetuating them.

The People's Institute model asserts that equitable communities and institutions can only be established and sustained by ethically sound organizers working together with intelligence, integrity and vision. The program requires all its trainers to struggle with and work through issues of racism and difficulties of organizing within their own communities. It also prides itself on being rooted in and accountable to communities of color.

Training Methods

The training model and analysis of racism is consistent across groups and situations, though trainers often use different examples to illustrate their points depending on the participant group. The trainings are clearly structured and use a format of engaging presentations

3. Chisom, R. & Washington, M. (1997). *Undoing racism: A philosophy of international social change*. The People's Institute Press.

and large group discussion. The People's Institute does not have a written manual or packet of materials for participants describing the goals and methods of the training model, however a publication outlining the Undoing Racism analytical framework is available.

> *"The way we structure our exercises and methodology comes straight from the street— straight from the community. We bring it with the spirit of the community."*

Initial training exercises help participants begin thinking "outside the box" and using a critical lens to examine social structures and dynamics. The training model uses the "foot of oppression" as a metaphor to describe the relationships between institutions, race and poverty. Trainers review important historical dates, legislation, people and policies that have impacted the development of institutional racism in the U.S. They talk about the role of institutional gatekeepers and the increased need for accountability to the communities that institutions serve. Internalized inferiority and superiority are also discussed as important factors maintaining community oppression and fostering social programs based on blame, punishment and denial. The training model explores language and definitions for understanding racism and examines how traditional views of intergroup relations such as "melting pot" theories and "colorblind" policies have ignored and denied racism in the U.S. Final discussions focus on community and institutional transformation and the leadership role of participants after the training.

THEORY OF CHANGE

The program fosters new understandings of racism by educating participants with a common analytical framework that can become the basis for a unified, anti-racism social movement.

Identifying and understanding structural racism is seen as the critical ingredient to successful community organizing against it. Communities are able to develop their own creative solutions, as well as practical methods for achieving them, once they have a clear problem analysis. Empowering participants, instilling hope, and developing accountable leadership are also important vehicles for establishing a multi-racial, liberation movement.

DISTINGUISHING FEATURES

The People's Institute is one of the few existing programs in the U.S. that focuses on institutional and structural forms of racism. The model makes important distinctions between individual expressions of prejudice, bias and discrimination, and institutional or systemic forms of racism. It critiques the dominance of individual-level approaches that fail to address the more prevalent, less visible, systemic dimensions of racism. The model challenges whites and people of color alike to recognize and work against those systems that provide unearned privilege to some and impose undeserved restrictions on others. It also encourages a race-based analysis of important social issues and institutions.

Over the past twenty years, the People's Institute training model has evolved based on experiences within communities across the U.S. The model is particularly strong in its grounding in and accountability to the communities it serves. The program is also both unusual and effective in providing both content and methods that are reflective of and appealing to many communities of color.

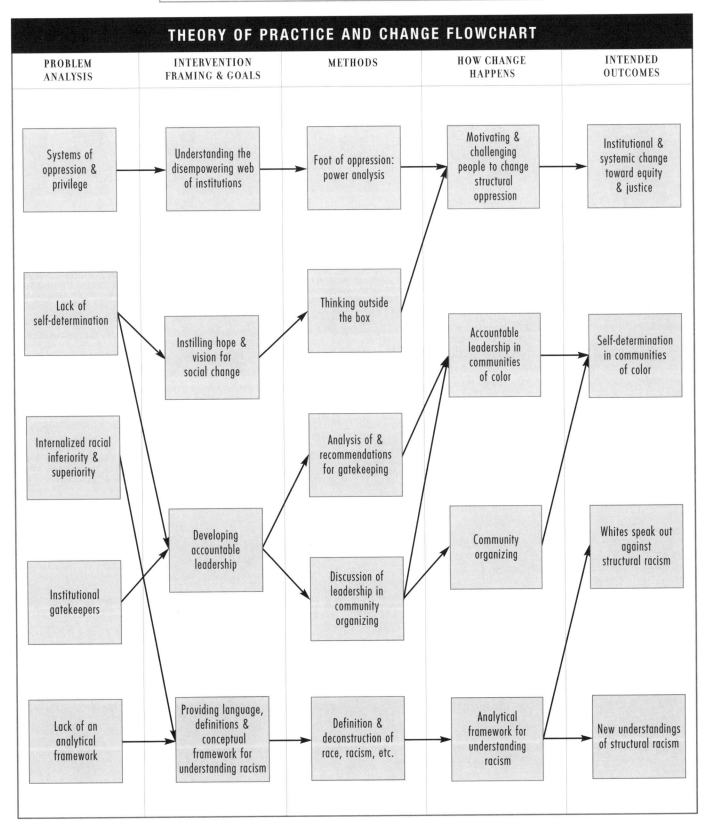

THEORY OF PRACTICE AND CHANGE FLOWCHART

PROBLEM ANALYSIS	INTERVENTION FRAMING & GOALS	METHODS	HOW CHANGE HAPPENS	INTENDED OUTCOMES
Systems of oppression & privilege	Understanding the disempowering web of institutions	Foot of oppression: power analysis	Motivating & challenging people to change structural oppression	Institutional & systemic change toward equity & justice
Lack of self-determination	Instilling hope & vision for social change	Thinking outside the box	Accountable leadership in communities of color	Self-determination in communities of color
Internalized racial inferiority & superiority	Developing accountable leadership	Analysis of & recommendations for gatekeeping	Community organizing	Whites speak out against structural racism
Institutional gatekeepers		Discussion of leadership in community organizing		
Lack of an analytical framework	Providing language, definitions & conceptual framework for understanding racism	Definition & deconstruction of race, racism, etc.	Analytical framework for understanding racism	New understandings of structural racism

2

NATIONAL COALITION BUILDING INSTITUTE

*"You don't change

people's minds,

you change

their hearts.

And you change

their hearts

through stories."*

NATIONAL COALITION BUILDING INSTITUTE

SUMMARY INFORMATION

ORGANIZATIONAL FOCUS	**Problem:** Prejudice, stereotypes, oppression, internalized oppression, separation. **Solution:** Healing, prejudice reduction, coalition building, leadership development, conflict resolution.
ORGANIZATIONAL HISTORY & CONTEXT	Founded in 1984 by Cherie Brown. Rooted in re-evaluation or co-counseling theory. Mission: "To end the mistreatment of every group whether it stems from nationality, race, class, gender, religion, sexual orientation, age, physical ability, job, or life circumstance."
THEORY OF PRACTICE	Prejudice Reduction.
ORGANIZATIONAL CAPACITY	Fifty community-based chapters, thirty non-profit and corporate affiliates, forty college campus chapters.
SERVICES	One, two and three-day Prejudice Reduction and Conflict Resolution workshop. Five-day Leadership Training Institute. Ongoing consultation or technical assistance when requested.
TYPES OF PARTICIPANTS	Diverse racial, gender, age, professional background and level of leadership. Community organizations and leaders, women's organizations, educators and students, law enforcement groups, unions, disabled people's organizations and corporations.
LEVEL OF ANALYSIS	Individuals and Intergroup.
PROBLEM ANALYSIS	Prejudice and discrimination come from early psychological hurts, fears and disempowerment; intergroup stereotypes and oppression; internalized oppression; habituated patterns of interaction; and polarization between groups.
INTERVENTION PRINCIPLES	Reducing prejudice, healing ourselves and others, and building coalitions requires that people become aware of early wounding and existing prejudices; express emotions in a supportive environment; develop compassion and support through hearing stories of others' oppression; and become empowered through skill-building and leadership development.
INTERVENTION METHODS	Standard training model for all groups that is flexible depending on group dynamics. Variety of learning tools including experiential exercises, presentations, small and larger group discussion, role-play. Clear, detailed and systematic materials and manuals.
INTENDED OUTCOMES	Change prejudicial attitudes. Individual healing and self-awareness. Re-humanize others. Appreciate differences. Change oppressive and conflict behaviors. Empower individuals. Develop leadership. Build coalition among individuals and groups.
THEORY OF CHANGE	Individual change comes from self-awareness, emotional discharge, and new skills and behavioral options. Relationship change comes from hearing people's experiences of oppression, recognizing common ground, and building alliances and coalitions.
CONTACT INFORMATION	Director: Cherie Brown 1835 K Street, N.W., Suite 715, Washington, DC 20006 phone: 202-785-9400 www.ncbi.org

Mission & History

Cherie Brown founded NCBI in 1984 with a mission to "...end the mistreatment of every group whether it stems from nationality, race, class, gender, religion, sexual orientation, age, physical ability, job, or life circumstance." NCBI's early work focused on reducing prejudice and building alliances between African American and Jewish community members, however, it quickly expanded to include many other groups. The program now concentrates on reducing individual-level prejudices, fostering interpersonal and inter-group alliances, building skills to empower leaders, and addressing controversial public issues. The program fits clearly within the prejudice reduction theory of practice.

NCBI traces its approach to the theories of re-evaluation counseling and psychoanalysis, which hold that distressing childhood experiences around our own and others' group identity create oppressive patterns of thought and behavior. Through processes of emotional discharge such as raging, crying, or laughing people can become more aware of their own patterns, more trusting of others, and better able to act successfully against oppression.

Organizational Capacity

NCBI currently has over 50 community-based chapters, 30 non-profit and corporate affiliates, and more than 40 college campus chapters. Most of its work is conducted in the U.S., however the organization also has chapters in Canada and Europe and has offered workshops around the world. NCBI offers one-, two- and three-day Prejudice Reduction and Conflict Resolution workshops, a five-day Leadership Training

---

SETTING THE SCENE

ON A WARM Saturday afternoon, 25 people are gathered in what otherwise might be an official-looking conference room at the Baltimore Hilton. The tables have been pushed back against the walls and the participants—a kaleidoscope of color, age and gender—are sitting in a semi-circle, eyes intent on the female participant and trainer who stand facing each other, hands locked together, at the front of the room. This group of local community leaders, church ministers, social workers, teachers, NGO leaders and others from the Washington D.C.-Baltimore area are gathered for a two-day prejudice reduction workshop offered by the National Coalition Building Institute (NCBI).

Now, at the end of the first day, a volunteer participant stands with the trainer in front of the group to demonstrate a "Speak Out"—an exercise about the healing power of personal stories of oppression. She tells a moving story about overhearing a conversation between her boss and a co-worker in which she was racially stereotyped and falsely accused. When the trainer encourages her to vent and say the least polite thing that comes to mind—something she really would have liked to say to her boss and co-worker—the tears and anger in her voice are mirrored by the furrowed brows and nodding heads of the other participants in the room who are watching her. They are with her, supporting her, as she recalls this incident and is encouraged by the trainer to say anything else she wants to in order to feel proud about sharing this experience with the group. They applaud her courage in sharing this story and raise their hands as one when the trainer asks who among them will make a commitment to fight against racial oppression in the workplace. Then several participants from the group share what the story brought up for them from their own lives, and the room begins to feel smaller, the group more intimate, than it did fifteen minutes before.

"The most horrible part of oppression," explains the trainer, "is that it silences our voices." This exercise is one of many NCBI uses to give voice to those who feel that they are least, lost, left out, discounted, disrespected, or dismissed. "Sharing and hearing stories of oppression," the trainer suggests, "helps heal personal wounds and open others' hearts to a place where compassion lives." This exercise may offer a new and different experience for each of the participants in the workshop, but it is a typical part of the many Prejudice Reduction and Leadership trainings that NCBI conducts within communities across the U.S.

Institute, and ongoing consultation or technical assistance where requested. The three-and five-day training programs also serve as training-of-trainers programs when participants learn how to conduct NCBI workshops.

Because NCBI requires all participants and trainers using their methods and materials to become affiliated with and pay fees to the organization, its human and financial base has expanded exponentially in a relatively short time. This innovative infrastructure has been an effective model for creating strong organizational capacity and sustainability. In addition, it has required NCBI to develop highly structured, clearly articulated training models and detailed materials to enable new trainers to learn NCBI's theory and methods in a relatively short time.

Types of Participants

NCBI offers training and consultation to a broad range of groups including community organizations and leaders, women's organizations, educators and students, law enforcement groups, unions, disabled people's organizations, and corporations. Trainings are open to all levels of leadership but usually focus at the grassroots level. NCBI does not believe in a hierarchy of oppression and holds that welcoming diversity must include all visible and invisible differences. The program works primarily with mixed or diverse identity groups. It also offers specialized trainings to groups from particular professions (e.g., police officers) or sectors (e.g., corporations).

UNDERSTANDING & INTERVENING IN PREJUDICE & OPPRESSION

Understanding the Problem

NCBI has a strong, psychological understanding of the causes of prejudice and oppression that focus on psychological wounding, learned stereotypes, internalized oppression, habituated patterns of thought and behavior, and group polarization. A basic assumption of this work is that people have been hurt, systematically mistreated, or convinced that they don't have power and this causes them to hurt others or perpetuate the mistreatment: because people are victims, they unconsciously victimize others. The program suggests that misinformation about one's own and others' identity groups learned from family, friends and media, among other sources, exert a powerful unconscious influence on people's thoughts and actions. In addition to causing discrimination and oppression of others, these negative messages and stereotypes can also become a constant internal critique that makes people ashamed, afraid or angry about their own group identity and causes them to perpetuate oppression within their own group. If unexamined, these early patterns of thought and behavior can become habituated and inflexible, decreasing people's ability to find new and creative ways of addressing prejudice and oppression. Finally, separation and polarization of identity groups keeps people focused on differences rather than common ground and creates opportunities for misunderstanding and conflict.

Addressing the Problem

The NCBI training model suggests that the best way to address these problems is to identify stereotypes people have learned and internalized about their own and others' groups, tell stories of personal experiences both of being a victim and of oppressing others, express pride in their own group, learn skills that empower people and give them options to habituated patterns, and build alliances between both individuals and groups. Trainings are based on the premise that once something is noticed it is changed forever. Surfacing unconscious beliefs and internal records about one's own and others' groups is an important part of personal growth and change. In keeping with the understanding that "guilt is the glue that holds prejudice in place," the program avoids blaming, condemning and moralizing and tries to maintain a hopeful and upbeat tone. It also tries to minimize competing feelings of victimization (i.e., "my group has suffered more than yours") by encouraging individuals to put aside their own pain when trying to help heal others. NCBI trainers explain that healing comes through sharing personal stories of oppression and emotional discharge such as yelling, crying and shaking. In addition, they seek to develop practical skills that empower people to effectively address prejudice, oppression and conflict. The program helps create new leadership in fighting prejudice and break old patterns of criticizing and attacking those who try to organize and promote community change.

NCBI's long-term goals include individual healing, rehumanizing others, appreciating differences, building connections with oneself and others, empowering individuals, and developing leadership for continued prejudice reduction and anti-oppression work.

Training Methods

NCBI trainings are highly structured, draw explicitly on adult learning principles, and include a variety of training methods including experiential exercises, presentations, large and small group discussion, identity group caucuses, role plays and skills practice. Initial exercises focus on identifying and appreciating the diversity in the training group, and both recognizing and challenging people's tendency to make connections with those who are similar or familiar rather than with those who are different from them. Additional exercises elicit both unconscious and conscious stereotypes people have internalized about their own and others' groups, and discourage blame and judgment about knowing these stereotypes. The program encourages participants to identify things that make them feel both ashamed and proud of their own group.

> " *The NCBI model allows people to see the importance of their individual initiative in bringing about institutional or societal change.*"

The model also works with group caucuses to identify and share what group members never want people to say, think, or do toward their group. This becomes preparation for "speak outs" or personal stories of oppression that are designed to help individuals discharge painful or angry emotions, and build compassion and support among participants for fighting different forms of oppression. Finally, trainings focus on developing and practicing skills for interrupting prejudicial comments, slurs or jokes and resolving interpersonal conflicts. Through role-plays and simulations, participants learn to identify underlying hurts, fears, concerns and needs that motivate people to make prejudicial remarks or take a particular position on a controversial issue. The model suggests that treating others with respect and decreasing defensiveness when confronted with prejudice or conflict can lead to productive conversations that foster either attitude change or a recognition of options for resolving conflicts.

THEORY OF CHANGE

NCBI suggests that individual level change comes through self-awareness or consciousness, emotional discharge, and skills practice in a supportive environment. Interpersonal and intergroup change occurs through sharing personal stories, rehumanizing the "other," fostering compassion and building inclusive networks and alliances. Leadership development and coalition building are the primary methods by which the NCBI model hopes to impact institutional changes. There is an implicit understanding that social institutions and systems are created and run by individuals and small groups, and that change must take place one person at a time.

DISTINGUISHING FEATURES

Unlike many of the other programs in the field, the NCBI model works directly with the emotional dimensions of prejudice and oppression. It takes a strong, holistic view of personal change and development, integrating attitudinal, emotional and behavioral dimensions of prejudice reduction. The model is also unusual in teaching practical skills for resolving conflict and interrupting interpersonal manifestations of prejudice such as racial jokes, slurs and comments. NCBI also addresses important issues of leadership oppression by fostering compassionate and supportive attitudes toward community leaders and breaking old patterns of criticizing or attacking those who try to organize and promote community change.

Drawing explicitly upon adult learning principles, NCBI trainings use active and varied

> *"I think one thing that sets the NCBI model apart from others is that we are willing to look the dragon in the eye— the fear, rage, hurt and anxiety, the guilt, the shame, where people have been set up to think of themselves and others as less than human. We look at that."*

methods that are conducive to many different individual and cultural learning styles. NCBI's theory of practice is well developed and both detailed and clearly structured in materials so that new trainers and participants can easily follow the connections between theory and practice. There is also a strong match between the program's "espoused theory"—what it says it does, and its "theory-in-use"—what it actually does. Finally, NCBI has a very strong training-of-trainers program and a well-developed infrastructure to support new trainers—a model that has proven to be effective in building organizational capacity and sustainability.

NATIONAL COALITION BUILDING INSTITUTE

THEORY OF PRACTICE AND CHANGE FLOWCHART

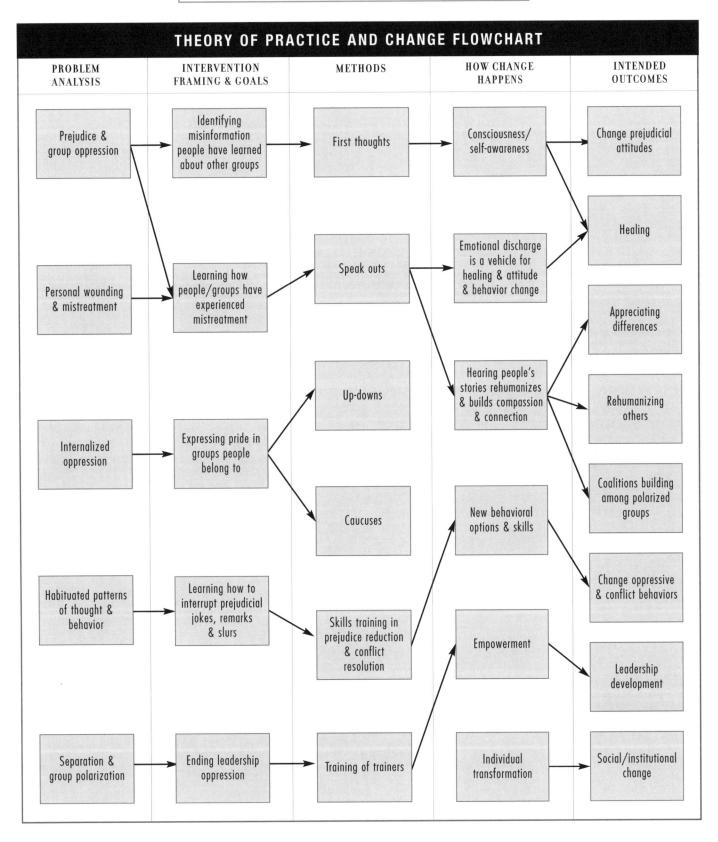

PROBLEM ANALYSIS	INTERVENTION FRAMING & GOALS	METHODS	HOW CHANGE HAPPENS	INTENDED OUTCOMES
Prejudice & group oppression	Identifying misinformation people have learned about other groups	First thoughts	Consciousness/ self-awareness	Change prejudicial attitudes
Personal wounding & mistreatment	Learning how people/groups have experienced mistreatment	Speak outs	Emotional discharge is a vehicle for healing & attitude & behavior change	Healing
Internalized oppression	Expressing pride in groups people belong to	Up-downs	Hearing people's stories rehumanizes & builds compassion & connection	Appreciating differences
		Caucuses		Rehumanizing others
			New behavioral options & skills	Coalitions building among polarized groups
Habituated patterns of thought & behavior	Learning how to interrupt prejudicial jokes, remarks & slurs	Skills training in prejudice reduction & conflict resolution	Empowerment	Change oppressive & conflict behaviors
				Leadership development
Separation & group polarization	Ending leadership oppression	Training of trainers	Individual transformation	Social/institutional change

VISIONS—VIGOROUS INTERVENTIONS INTO ONGOING NATURAL SETTINGS

> "*It is not our differences*
>
> *that divide us.*
>
> *It is our inability*
>
> *to recognize,*
>
> *accept and celebrate*
>
> *those differences.*"
>
> *Audre Lorde*

SUMMARY INFORMATION

ORGANIZATIONAL FOCUS	**Problem:** Modern racism, internalized oppression, monoculturalism, historic inequities. **Solution:** Multiculturalism, appreciating diversity, inclusion, equity, power sharing development, conflict resolution.
ORGANIZATIONAL HISTORY & CONTEXT	Founded in 1984 by three African American women and one white Jewish man from Rocky Mount, NC. Rooted in Clinical Psychodynamic, Transactional Analysis and Gestalt theories. Mission: "to pass on respect for group and individual differences and faith in the potential of equitable institutions."
THEORY OF PRACTICE	Diversity/Multiculturalism and Anti-Racism.
ORGANIZATIONAL CAPACITY	Two Regional Offices, ten Senior Consultants, eighteen to twenty Specialized Trainers and Consultants.
SERVICES	Four-Day "Changing Racism" workshop, Parts I, II, & III (being developed). Ongoing Multicultural Skills Building Group (advanced training of trainers). Customized training and community development contracts. Ongoing consultation and technical assistance when requested.
TYPES OF PARTICIPANTS	Community organizations and leaders, women's groups, people of color, corporations and businesses, mental health providers, social service providers, affirmative action officers, educators, political leaders, religious leaders, blue-collar workers and foundations.
LEVEL OF ANALYSIS	Individual and Structural.
PROBLEM ANALYSIS	Modern racism stems from unacknowledged historic legacies of inequity, learned patterns of oppression, monoculturalism, and negative messages about one's own and others' groups.
INTERVENTION PRINCIPLES	Recognizing, understanding and appreciating differences requires personal awareness and emotional literacy, recognizing cultural differences, changing social messages and attitudes, fostering "both/and" thinking, and recognizing change as an ongoing process.
INTERVENTION METHODS	Standard model for all groups that is flexible depending on group dynamics. Presentation, small group discussion, and experiential exercises as primary learning tools. Skillful facilitation of group dynamics and attention to individual participants' needs.
INTENDED OUTCOMES	Change in individual attitudes and behaviors. Develop emotional literacy; recognize and appreciate group differences. Understand impact of social oppression on individuals. Provide alternatives to survival behavior for modern racism and internalized oppression. Restructure power in organizations as indicated.
THEORY OF CHANGE	Awareness of one's own attitudes, emotions and behaviors; ongoing contact with own and other groups, recognizing and appreciating differences. Understanding behavioral alternatives. Ongoing or sustained work within communities and organizations resulting in redistributions of power at personal, interpersonal, institutional and cultural levels.
CONTACT INFORMATION	Director: Valerie Batts 17 Spring Valley Arlington, MA 02476 phone: 781-642-2291 WWW.VISIONS-Inc.com

Mission & History

Vigorous InterventionS In Ongoing Natural Settings (VISIONS) was established in 1984 by four "children of the 60's," including three African American women from Rocky Mount, North Carolina. Together they "…sought to pass on the respect for group and individual differences and faith in the potential of equitable institutions that they had learned in this small southern town." VISIONS provides an analysis that integrates personal, interpersonal, institutional and cultural expressions of modern racism and a practical focus on participants' personal understandings and experiences of diversity and racism.

The training model is grounded in existential psychology and community activist theories and techniques that promote personal growth and social change. Consultants use techniques from Transactional Analysis, Gestalt psychology and system theory as well as worldview analysis and other change models. The training model includes an analysis of individuals in their environments, a focus on here-and-now awareness and an emphasis on understanding "how" rather than "why" oppression occurs. The training model focuses on individual and systemic dimensions of racism and merges multiculturalism/diversity and anti-racism theories of practice.

Organizational Capacity

VISIONS currently has two regional offices located in Cambridge, MA, and Rocky Mount, NC, and provides a variety of multicultural trainings, program assessment, consulting and community development services. The program offers regularly scheduled four-day "Changing Racism" trainings that are open to the general public; an "Ongoing Multicultural Skills Building Group" for advanced, long-term, training-of-trainers; and individually designed contract trainings and consulting for communities and organizations.

SETTING THE SCENE

IN THE COMmunity room of a black Baptist church in rural North Carolina, the 30 participants in VISIONS "Changing Racism" training are meeting in two small groups in separate corners of the room. All of the participants are African American congregants age 45-65, except the church pastor, the white mayor of the town, a white local hospital nurse, and a white out-of-town guest.

All eyes are closed as the consultants in each group slowly remind participants to relax into the short meditation exercise. "Remember one of the first times you encountered someone from another race," suggests the trainer. "Picture the scene. What are you doing? What are you thinking about them? How does it end?" The community room is hushed for four or five minutes as participants recall these first experiences. Then the trainers ask participants to slowly open their eyes and come back to the group, bringing their memories with them.

"How did you feel about this early encounter?" the consultants ask each participant. They hand out a colorful chart entitled "The Feeling Wheel" and ask participants to identify their feelings of sadness, fear, anger, joy, peacefulness and powerfulness on the chart as they describe their memories. "How did that experience shape who you are now?" The trainers skillfully work with each participant over the next hour as they share their memories with the group.

While personal healing and identification of early messages is the initial focus of this exercise, consistent with VISIONS' integrative philosophy, the consultant soon takes the analysis one step further to initiate a group discussion about how individual experiences are shaped by existing institutions and power relations that perpetuate monoculturalism—the rejection or oppression of cultural differences—and racism. "To start a social movement that fights against racism and appreciates diversity, we have to start with ourselves," explains the consultant.

VISIONS has a racially, ethnically and culturally diverse group of 10 senior consultants and an additional 18-20 organizational consultants. These consultants have professional backgrounds in clinical, counseling and social psychology, law, education, business, organizational development, communication, health and community organizing. VISIONS has created a solid financial base from providing long-term training and consulting services to corporations. This work has helped diversify their program expertise and sustain their work in local community initiatives. The program stresses the importance of staying culturally, professionally and personally rooted in the beliefs of its founders and African American communities rather than fitting into traditional ideas about organizational development.

> *"A fish doesn't know it's in the water. That's what monoculturalism is. The dominant culture's task is to figure out where the water is."*

Types of Participants

The program provides trainings of varying lengths and focus areas to mental health providers, social service providers, affirmative action officers, educators, managers, health care providers, political leaders, religious leaders and blue-collar workers. VISIONS works with both mixed and separate racial groups and specializes in trainings for people of color and women. Trainers' backgrounds are matched to participants' backgrounds where possible in an effort to provide appropriate cultural interpretation and models.

While race relations and racism is an important part of VISIONS' multicultural work, the program focuses on similar dynamics among many forms of oppression and does not recognize a hierarchy among different forms of oppression. The model holds that creating a multicultural environment requires the understanding and elimination of different "isms" including: racism, sexism, ageism, classism, heterosexism, anti-Semitism, adultism and ableism.

UNDERSTANDING & INTERVENING IN RACISM & OPPRESSION

Understanding the Problem

VISIONS points to monoculturalism, unacknowledged historical legacies of inequity and learned patterns of oppression as the primary causes of modern racism. The program defines modern racism as unconsciously held beliefs and feelings that people of color are making illegitimate demands for changes in the status quo. It includes the attribution of non-race related reasons for behaviors that deny blacks and other targets of systemic oppression equal access to opportunities. Where "old-fashioned" racism involved overt behaviors, practices and attitudes of white superiority and black inferiority, modern racism reflects attitudes and practices that have been driven underground by changes in laws and norms. Modern racism manifests itself in more subtle, symbolic and "invisible" forms of oppression and privilege.[4]

VISIONS integrates the analysis of personal racism—individual prejudice or bias; interpersonal racism—discriminatory behaviors toward people of color; institutional racism—policies, practices, laws and procedures that disadvantage people of color; and cultural racism—cultural oppression and rejection of differences. These forms of racism manifest in a number of dysfunctional behavior patterns among both dominant and non-dominant groups.

VISIONS model holds that one of the primary causes of modern racism is monoculturalism. Members of the dominant culture are often not even aware that mainstream definitions of what is "right" or "beautiful," "melting pot" theories of cultural assimilation and "colorblind" public policies serve to exclude or reject important cultural differences.

---

4. Batts, Valerie (1998, May). *Modern Racism: New Melody for the Same Old Tunes.* EDS Occasional Papers. Episcopal Divinity School.

Other sources of racism are unacknowledged, historic power imbalances and traditions of oppression and privilege that have been passed down from one generation to the next. The model looks at how oppression is socially learned and internalized. It outlines a number of behavioral patterns that may be important psychological or social survival strategies for coping with internalized oppression, but also block efforts to make effective social change.

Addressing the Problem

VISIONS' training model suggests that the best way to address these problems is to recognize and understand the different forms of modern racism, unlearn ingrained patterns of oppression, and foster multiculturalism or acceptance, appreciation, utilization and celebration of diversity. VISIONS psychosocial approach to changing racism emphasizes the importance of individual awareness and emotional literacy—or the ability to read one's own emotions and those of others—in the process of understanding and changing oppression. The model also helps participants recognize systemic and cultural forms of oppression and their impact on individuals' thoughts, emotions and behaviors. The program suggests that both individuals and institutions must take responsibility for creating a more equitable and just future.

"We do a lot of work around how to talk about racism at the cultural level. Who determines what's considered right and beautiful? Who sets the norms on what's appropriate behavior? How do people relate to each other?"

The model also highlights different groups' experiences of reality that must be included and legitimized in creating multicultural communities and workplaces. "Both/And" thinking requires that individuals accept differences rather than deny, shame or attack them and move beyond prevalent social dichotomies of "good/bad", "right/wrong" and "black/white".

Training Methods

In keeping with its focus on psychodynamic Transactional Analysis (TA) and Gestalt theories and methods, VISIONS' trainers often work closely with the group dynamics within the training. The focus on how participants interact with each other surfaces issues that often have deeper roots in unresolved racial problems. Here-and-now awareness also allows trainers to help participants understand, re-experience and ultimately resolve some of those issues.

Although the program does not yet have training manuals that integrate theory and practice, participants receive a packet of materials that includes core concepts, worksheets and insightful articles related to racism and multiculturalism. Participants are often assigned specified reading materials or other homework each evening in preparation for the following day's discussions. The tone of trainings is generally informal and upbeat, and learning tools include presentation, small-group discussion and experiential exercises.

The model begins by looking at how dysfunctional experiences provide important information about the impact of oppression. Trainers discuss both subjective and objective aspects of racism, violence and other forms of oppression.

Participants have the opportunity to identify both the target (oppressed) and non-target (privileged) groups to which they belong, and discuss personal experiences of being both the oppressed and the oppressor. In addition, trainers present statistics about racism and other "isms" in the U.S. to highlight the structural or systemic dimension of oppression. Exercises such as "first encounters" (which was described in Setting the Scene) help participants recognize social messages they may have internalized about other groups and provides an opportunity to discuss how early experiences have shaped current attitudes or relationships.

Participants have the opportunity to caucus with other members of their target group to identify aspects of their culture that make them proud and ways they have been impacted by "isms." Through presentations and group discussions, VISIONS presents a series of alternative behaviors for dealing with modern "isms" and internalized oppression. Finally, trainers focus on the power of positive feedback and encourage participants to identify positive characteristics of people who are different from them as practice for appreciating diversity. This process also teaches people how to question previous training to prefer sameness.

THEORY OF CHANGE

VISIONS outlines a three-stage process of change toward multiculturalism. Different groups may begin at different stages in the process. The first stage involves recognizing personal biases including negative perceptions of both oneself and others who do not fit into the accepted norm. This norm is generally based on non-target groups (i.e. white, male, age 25 to 45, heterosexual, U.S. born, English speaking, Protestant, middle class and physically able). The second step involves validating cultural differences and valuing diversity with "...explicit attention to power sharing, redistribution of resources and redefinition of what is right and beautiful at all levels." Finally, the process involves a willingness to experiment with new behaviors and ongoing contact with members of one's own and other groups. While the relationship between individual and social oppression is highlighted in VISIONS' analysis, change is viewed as typically beginning at the individual level. Strong individual leaders and multi-cultural coalitions work together to create social change toward equity and multiculturalism.

DISTINGUISHING FEATURES

VISIONS' analytical framework provides a sophisticated and insightful integration of different levels of analysis and theories of practice. The model examines individual, interpersonal and systemic forms of oppression from the perspective of psychological impacts of oppression, cultural differences, and social, political and economic power imbalances. VISIONS' training model recognizes the multi-faceted, complex dynamics of racism and racial conflict.

It also directly addresses the role of emotions in unlearning racism and overcoming internalized oppression. VISIONS' consultants and trainers draw upon their experience in clinical psychology and demonstrate considerable skill and flexibility in working with the different needs and experiences of participants in their trainings.

VISIONS also provides a unique model of program development that is rooted in the cultural, professional and personal experiences of its founders. Its organic development has insured a consistent quality of experienced trainers and facilitators. While the slow growth of the organization may have limited its capacity to train large numbers of people, the program has maintained strong credibility in a variety of different settings and sectors (e.g., corporate, non-profit and community work) and been successful in sustaining its efforts over time.

VISIONS—VigorouS InterventionS into Ongoing Natural Settings

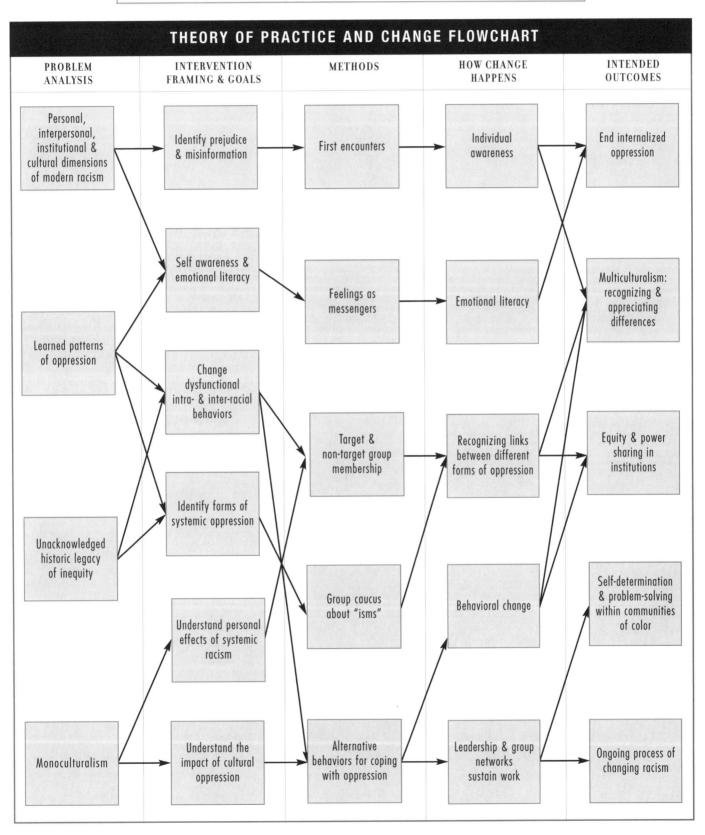

THEORY OF PRACTICE AND CHANGE FLOWCHART

PROBLEM ANALYSIS	INTERVENTION FRAMING & GOALS	METHODS	HOW CHANGE HAPPENS	INTENDED OUTCOMES
Personal, interpersonal, institutional & cultural dimensions of modern racism	Identify prejudice & misinformation	First encounters	Individual awareness	End internalized oppression
Learned patterns of oppression	Self awareness & emotional literacy	Feelings as messengers	Emotional literacy	Multiculturalism: recognizing & appreciating differences
	Change dysfunctional intra- & inter-racial behaviors	Target & non-target group membership	Recognizing links between different forms of oppression	Equity & power sharing in institutions
Unacknowledged historic legacy of inequity	Identify forms of systemic oppression	Group caucus about "isms"	Behavioral change	Self-determination & problem-solving within communities of color
	Understand personal effects of systemic racism			
Monoculturalism	Understand the impact of cultural oppression	Alternative behaviors for coping with oppression	Leadership & group networks sustain work	Ongoing process of changing racism

WORLD OF DIFFERENCE® INSTITUTE—
ANTI-DEFAMATION LEAGUE

"Prejudice is learned

and can be unlearned...

With awareness,

education and action,

we can weed it out."

ADL, 1998

WORLD OF DIFFERENCE® INSTITUTE—Anti-Defamation League

SUMMARY INFORMATION

ORGANIZATIONAL FOCUS	**Problem:** Bias, bigotry, stereotypes, discrimination, hatred, racism, anti-Semitism. **Solution:** Diversity awareness, anti-bias, intergroup relations, pluralism, tolerance, dialogue.
ORGANIZATIONAL HISTORY & CONTEXT	Founded in 1985 as an Anti-Defamation League program. Rooted in social learning, educational and cultural theories. Mission: "To combat prejudice, promote democratic ideals and strengthen pluralism."
THEORY OF PRACTICE	Diversity/Multiculturalism.
ORGANIZATIONAL CAPACITY	Thirty regional chapters. Extensive curricula, publications and videos available.
SERVICES	Custom-designed, anti-bias and diversity awareness trainings for communities schools, universities and businesses. Ongoing consultation or technical assistance when requested.
TYPES OF PARTICIPANTS	Social service workers, volunteers and staff of community organizations, civic leaders, youth, educators, police and corporations.
LEVEL OF ANALYSIS	Individuals and Intergroup.
PROBLEM ANALYSIS	People learn bias and discrimination from family, friends, media, social institutions, cultural messages and social norms. Dominant groups exclude, deny or denigrate cultural differences and feel threatened by the growing number of "minorities" in the U.S.
INTERVENTION PRINCIPLES	Anti-bias and diversity awareness work involves becoming aware of personal and social biases, valuing or appreciating differences, making a critical examination of widespread social messages about stereotypes and discrimination, developing skills for communicating across cultures, and planning individual and collective action to make change in community and workplace environments.
INTERVENTION METHODS	Flexible model based on group needs. Variety of learning tools including experiential exercises, presentations, small and larger group discussion, role-play, videos, etc. Clear and innovative materials and manuals.
INTENDED OUTCOMES	Change individuals' biased attitudes and discriminatory behavior. Develop awareness of cultural differences. Critically examine social messages and practices that create bias and discrimination. Teach non-discriminatory communication skills. Foster inclusive, tolerant and diverse communities, schools and workplaces.
THEORY OF CHANGE	Self-awareness. New behavioral options. Critical examination of social messages. New knowledge and appreciation of cultural differences. Individual change and action.
CONTACT INFORMATION	Director: Lindsay Friedman 309 W. Washington, Suite 750, Chicago, IL 60606 phone: 312-782-5080

Mission & History

Responding to racial integration problems in Boston schools, the Anti-Defamation League (ADL)[5] launched the World of Difference® Institute in 1985 as an anti-bias and diversity awareness program designed "...to combat prejudice, promote democratic ideals and strengthen pluralism." The program offers a variety of trainings and an extensive array of materials to raise awareness about the destructive effects of bias and discrimination, and provides strategies and resources for working with diversity in U.S. communities, schools and workplaces.

The World of Difference® Institute began as an anti-bias educational campaign in Massachusetts schools involving television, radio and newspaper messages, teacher-training and curricula development, and community events. The program quickly expanded beyond its school-based origins into community and workplace settings.

Drawing on social learning, cultural and education theories, the World of Difference® Institute holds that people learn prejudicial attitudes and discriminatory behavior early and unconsciously through the imitation of role models. In addition, fear and ignorance of cultural differences can perpetuate misinterpretation, misunderstanding and intergroup tensions. The training model uses cooperative, active learning processes and principles to address problems of exclusion, intolerance and denigration of

---

SETTING THE SCENE

THE ATRIUM Ballroom at the Washington Court Hotel is half-filled with 10-12 banquet tables and a diverse group of 45 people, including human resource managers, high school teachers, police officers and representatives from local community organizations. Gathered for the Anti-Defamation League's World of Difference® Institute, these participants now sit quietly, listening closely to the 2 trainers give instructions for an exercise called "Name Five." The trainers check their watches and tell participants that they have three minutes to quickly write down the names of 5 prominent Americans in the first of twelve boxes in their answer grid. Many of the participants look down at their answer sheet and appear eager to get started on this test of knowledge.

"Time!" calls one of the trainers and quickly resets his watch for another three minutes, "Now write down the names of 5 prominent American men in the second box." Some participants look confused for a moment, realizing that they had unwittingly filled their first box only with prominent men.

"Time!" calls the trainer and resets his watch yet again. The three-minute time limits continue as participants are asked to list 5 prominent members of additional groups for each box in the grid including: American women; African Americans; Latino Americans; Asian/Pacific Islander Americans; Native Americans; Jewish Americans; Roman Catholic Americans; lesbian, gay, or bisexual Americans; Americans with disabilities; and Americans over 65.

When the final time limit is called, participants look around surprised and a bit nervous; many have a sinking feeling that they have failed an important test. The trainers ask if anyone was able to fill in all of the boxes of their answer grid. No one raises a hand. In fact, only 3-4 people have been able to fill in more than eight of the answer grids completely.

"What makes someone prominent?" asks the trainer. "What sources did you think of in writing down your answers?" "Would it help if you could collaborate with others in filling out this grid next time?"

These questions provoke a discussion about who people know, how they know what they know, where they get their information, and where they go for new information. Trainers soon broaden the discussion to explore how people's limited frames of reference impact their communities and workplaces. Participants are actively engaged and many experience "aha" moments of insight as they begin to question some of their assumptions, and critically examine social messages about racial, ethnic and cultural groups.

---

5. The Anti-Defamation League is a civil rights and human relations agency established in 1913 to "secure justice and fair treatment to all citizens alike and to put an end forever to unjust and unfair discrimination against and ridicule of any sect or body of citizens."

diverse individuals and groups. World of Difference® Institute fits well within the diversity and multicultural theory of practice.

Organizational Capacity

Over the past sixteen years, the program has grown to operate in 29 U.S. cities and 14 countries around the world. It has expanded beyond its original audiences of schools and youth (Classroom of Difference®) to include components for college and university students, faculty and staff (Campus of Difference™), corporate, small business and non-profit organizations (Workplace of Difference™) and community and law enforcement organizations (Community of Difference™).

The World of Difference® Institute provides six-hour, twelve-hour, eighteen-hour and forty-hour customized trainings as well as ongoing consulting or technical assistance to organizations, institutions and communities across the country. In conjunction with these services, the program offers extensive and innovative resource materials on issues of bias and diversity.

This program is considered an educational, preventive and proactive arm of the ADL. Drawing upon the ADL as an organizational base, the World of Difference® Institute has become one of the most recognizable and widely-used national diversity and anti-bias training programs in the U.S.

Types of Participants

The program offers training primarily to communities, businesses, or schools that express an interest in learning skills and knowledge to help manage and value their growing diversity. The community-based section of the program works with a variety of groups including: social service workers, volunteers and staff of community organizations, civic leaders and law enforcement professionals. The trainings usually involve racially, ethnically or culturally mixed groups. Many of the programs are customized to address issues and concerns about bias and diversity within specific professions. For example, the Community of Difference® program has developed specialized exercises and training materials for working with law enforcement personnel such as police cadets, experienced officers and civilian personnel in police departments.

UNDERSTANDING & INTERVENING IN DIVERSITY & OPPRESSION

Understanding the Problem

World of Difference® Institute focuses on social psychological and cultural factors that foster prejudicial attitudes and discriminatory behaviors in individuals, and cause racial and ethnic tensions between groups. The training model suggests that bias and discrimination are socially learned as children imitate the attitudes and behaviors modeled by their family, friends and teachers. Reinforced by pervasive social norms, cultural messages and institutional policies and practices, people often indirectly and unconsciously learn to associate particular ethnic, racial or cultural groups with power and privilege, and others with such things as crime, violence, poverty and drug addiction. The World of Difference® Institute model suggests that this early social learning is very difficult to unlearn.

The Institute's training model also holds that members of the dominant culture are often not interested in or sensitive to cultural differences and tend to ignore or exclude those who do not act, think, or look like they do. In addition, dominant groups may feel threatened by changing U.S. demographics and fear losing their place or status in communities and workplaces. The result can be increased intolerance, inequity and conflict between what has traditionally been referred to as "majority" and "minority" groups. The growing diversity in U.S. communities that will inevitably change the status quo of intergroup relations makes it increasingly important to develop effective strategies for different identity groups to successfully live and work together.

Addressing the Problem

The World of Difference® Institute training model suggests that the first step in addressing these problems is to identify or recognize one's own biased attitudes and discriminatory behaviors. In addition to promoting self-awareness, the training model also develops skills for critically examining social messages and practices that foster, oppression and for challenging or openly criticizing bias and bigotry. Trainings also provide basic skills and language for communicating effectively and respectfully across cultures.

The World of Difference® Institute educates participants about cultural differences to encourage the appreciation of diversity. While the model presents some facts and information about different identity groups, the primary focus is on exploring similarities and differences among participants' own cultures and applying those understandings to cultural diversity where participants live and work. The trainings also try to build empathy among participants and enhance both individual self-esteem and pride in their cultural heritage. The model suggests that people who feel good about themselves do not need to denigrate others.

> *"One of the most important things we can do for people is to help them look at social messages, evaluate them, and ask, "I wonder where I could find out another point of view?" Or, "how might this be presented differently by a different group of people?"*

The World of Difference® Institute training model focuses on being inclusive and expanding the idea of diversity. Practitioners often mention inequities between groups and the uniqueness of different forms of bigotry, however they do not suggest that one form of oppression (e.g., racism or sexism) is more important than another. The model discourages participants from competing for victim status and suggests that no one group's pain is more legitimate than another.

Training Methods

The World of Difference® Institute has extensive materials for use with different groups and situations including a broad spectrum of experiential exercises and games, case studies, video vignettes for discussion, simulations or role-plays, discussion questions and curricula. Based on an initial needs assessment, the trainers design an agenda to fit each group. However, the structure of trainings consistently focuses first on issues of identity, then on culture, and finally on bias. In addition, the trainings generally begin with developing awareness and new knowledge, and later move to action and the application of new learning. Trainings are highly structured and include a variety of learning tools and methods that are designed to encourage participants' self-discovery rather than pre-determined training points. The World of Difference® Institute training model utilizes adult learning principles in drawing attention to individual learning needs and styles, developing particpatory or active learning strategies, practically applying newly learned information, skills, or attitudes, and valuing participants' knowledge and experience.

Initial exercises in the training focus on participants' own sense of identity and highlight the diversity represented in the training group. Additional exercises help participants examine unconscious stereotypes and develop a critical perspective about the social messages people receive about specific cultural groups in the U.S. Video vignettes of individual bias (e.g., jokes, comments, or slurs), cultural bias (e.g., ways of communicating or acting that are viewed as credible), and institutional bias (e.g., companies' hiring and promotion practices) provide a common platform for discussion. This section of the training may also include a brief skill-building section on non-discriminatory communication or basic conflict resolution methods. The final section of the training usually includes some form of community needs assessment, action planning, and application of learning from the training to the community or workplace. It also encourages participants to form collaborative alliances across racial, ethnic and cultural lines to promote community change.

THEORY OF CHANGE

The World of Difference® Institute suggests that individual attitude change comes through self awareness, a critical analysis of social messages and norms, and new information about cultural differences. Individual behavioral change follows from these changed attitudes and from the development of new skills for effective interaction in diverse communities and workplaces.

Improved intergroup relations result from appreciative attitudes about diversity and respectful interaction between different groups. Building empathy between individuals and groups and improving both personal and collective self-esteem also fosters improved intergroup relations. Finally, individuals and cooperative groups

"It's definitely not a one size fits all program. We have so many possible programs and exercises to choose from... The training exercises really depend on what the topic is, participants' level of experience, or the intensity of the situation."

valuing diversity within their own personal and professional spheres of influence serve as the vehicle for changing institutions and social messages.

DISTINGUISHING FEATURES

Drawing on the ADL's human and financial resources and long-standing, positive reputation in the areas of civil rights and anti-discrimination work, the World of Difference® Institute is able to reach a large number of people. In addition, the program's emphasis on social learning theories, appreciating diversity, and individual and intergroup levels of analysis, makes its message and goals accessible and acceptable to a variety of community, workplace and classroom settings. The World of Difference® Institute's training programs are custom designed based on the needs of participants and supplemented with very innovative and well-developed training materials. Exercises focus on "showing" rather than "telling" participants about prejudice and discrimination, and draw upon adult learning research. Because materials are only available in conjunction with training or consulting services, the program is able to maintain consistency and quality control in program implementation.

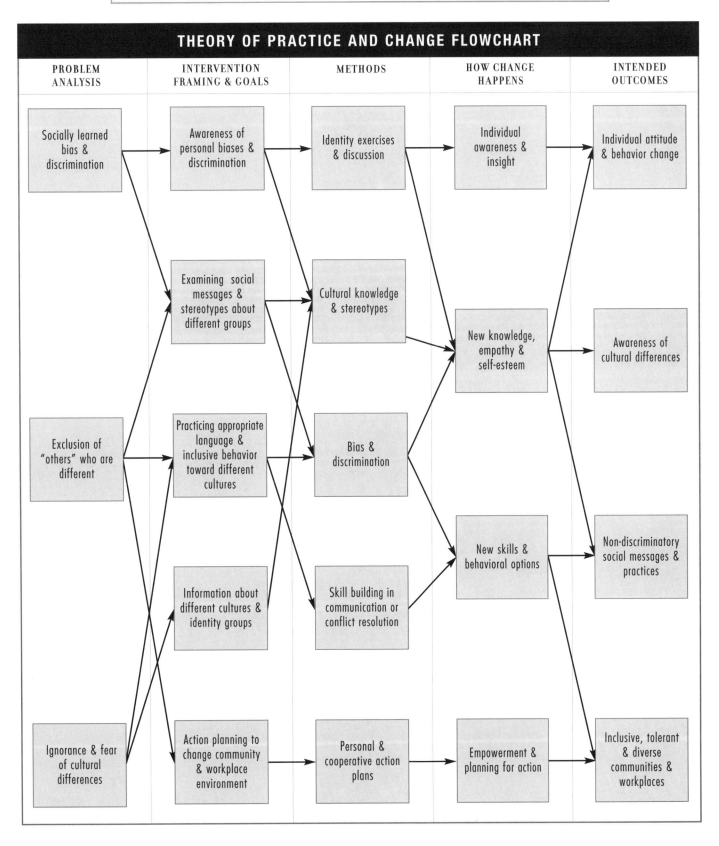

THEORY OF PRACTICE AND CHANGE FLOWCHART

PROBLEM ANALYSIS	INTERVENTION FRAMING & GOALS	METHODS	HOW CHANGE HAPPENS	INTENDED OUTCOMES
Socially learned bias & discrimination	Awareness of personal biases & discrimination	Identity exercises & discussion	Individual awareness & insight	Individual attitude & behavior change
	Examining social messages & stereotypes about different groups	Cultural knowledge & stereotypes	New knowledge, empathy & self-esteem	Awareness of cultural differences
Exclusion of "others" who are different	Practicing appropriate language & inclusive behavior toward different cultures	Bias & discrimination	New skills & behavioral options	Non-discriminatory social messages & practices
	Information about different cultures & identity groups	Skill building in communication or conflict resolution		
Ignorance & fear of cultural differences	Action planning to change community & workplace environment	Personal & cooperative action plans	Empowerment & planning for action	Inclusive, tolerant & diverse communities & workplaces

CROSSROADS MINISTRY

*"Community change
cannot take place
without internal
institutional transformation...
Institutions must be
a part of shaping a
movement for anti-racist
change in this country."*

CROSSROADS MINISTRY

ORGANIZATIONAL FOCUS	**Problem:** Institutional, cultural and systemic racism, historic oppression, internalized inferiority and superiority. **Solution:** Anti-racist institutional transformation, faith-based analysis of racism, anti-racist team leadership in institutions, racial equity and justice.
ORGANIZATIONAL HISTORY & CONTEXT	Co-founded in 1986 by a collective led by Reverend Joseph Barndt. Rooted in spiritual and faith-based anti-racism work and community organizing. Mission: "...to dismantle racism and build anti-racist multicultural diversity within institutions...through developing institutional transformation teams."
THEORY OF PRACTICE	Anti-Racism.
ORGANIZATIONAL CAPACITY	National office in Chicago. One additional office in Wisconsin. Ten trainers. Videotapes, books and music CDs for dismantling racism.
SERVICES	Three-phase team training process. Leadership development institute (training of trainers). Ongoing consulting and coaching for institutions when requested.
TYPES OF PARTICIPANTS	Religious, educational and other social service institutions committed to community change and justice issues.
LEVEL OF ANALYSIS	Structural.
PROBLEM ANALYSIS	Institutional racism stems from unexamined historic systems of racial privilege and oppression that continue to influence institutions' mission, purpose and means of control. Institutions lack internal racial analysis and accountability to the communities of color that they serve.
INTERVENTION PRINCIPLES	Anti-racist institutional change requires working with teams within the institution to analyze systemic racism and develop and implement strategies to dismantle racism within their structures and within the communities they serve.
INTERVENTION METHODS	Standard one-year training model with long-term institutional commitment. Presentation, small group exercises and discussion, video analysis and reflection on application as primary learning tools.
INTENDED OUTCOMES	New understandings of institutional and structural racism. Anti-racism leadership within institutions. Accountable policies and practices to communities of color. Institutional and community change toward equity and justice.
THEORY OF CHANGE	Institutional commitment to change. Internal change in institutional culture, identity and purpose. Racial-justice analytical framework. Accountable institutional leadership.
CONTACT INFORMATION	Co-Executive Directors: Robette Dias and Chuck Ruehle 425 South Central Park Avenue, Chicago, IL 60624 phone: 773-638-0166

Mission & History

Crossroads Ministry (Crossroads), an interfaith ministry for racial justice, was co-founded in 1986 by a collective led by Reverend Joseph Barndt with a mission to "...dismantle racism and build anti-racist multicultural diversity within institutions...through developing institutional transformation teams." Crossroads uses an analytical framework of racism that is similar to its sister organization, the People's Institute for Survival and Beyond, yet focuses on training anti-racism teams within institutions who can lead long-term, structural and programmatic transformation. Over the course of a year, institutional teams learn an analytical framework to talk about and work against racism, and develop an internal capacity and strategy for ongoing structural change. Crossroads' team-based model has evolved over twelve years of experience conducting anti-racism training in institutions and the communities they serve.

Like the People's Institute, Crossroads' training model has its roots in the civil rights and community organizing efforts of the 1960s and 1970s that provided skills and tools for community action against injustice. Crossroads brings a spiritual, faith-based approach to organizing against institutional racism. The model suggests that anti-racism work is about restoration: racism serves to divide the family of children that God created. Those doing anti-racism work are called upon to recognize and reunite the collective family. Trainers suggest that historically, many religious institutions have misused spiritual, biblical and sacred stories to perpetuate oppression and reinforce separation between individuals and groups. Crossroads invites participants to embark on

SETTING THE SCENE

IN A LARGE classroom in Nashville, Tennessee, 6 teams from different national churches have gathered for the first of Crossroads Ministry's three Anti-Racism Trainings for Institutional Change. These regional church teams consist of 5-7 members selected by their church to lead their institutions in anti-racism work over the next year. Each team now meets separately in different corners of the room to examine a handout of a continuum on becoming an anti-racist, multicultural institution. The continuum charts the characteristics and policies of institutions as they move from exclusive, monoculturalism where racial and cultural differences are seen as deficits, through symbolic and analytical change where institutions are tolerant or non-discriminatory, and finally to inclusive, anti-racist multicultural institutions where differences are seen as assets.

As participants discuss the differences along the continuum, a quiet argument begins in one small group. "We are clearly an 'awakening institution,'" argues a middle aged woman. "I think we've done a great job being sensitive to differences and wanting to eliminate discriminatory practices. But we are still conforming to white people's norms, worldviews and practices. We have a long way to go to really being inclusive of cultural differences."

"I think you are being overly optimistic, Miriam," comments another woman in the group. "We still act like a 'club institution.' Sure we are tolerant of some diversity, but only if those from different backgrounds have the right perspective and credentials. Most of the congregants don't think we have a problem. That's part of the problem right there."

"I think you are both right," a young man from the same group chimes in. "It seems that almost everyone in the church believes we are at that awakening stage...we talk like we are there already...we like to think we are there. But really, when you look closely at our informal practices, decision-making methods and policies, we seem to be two steps behind our rhetoric. We are really a club."

The conversation in all of the small groups becomes more intense as the hour continues and group members offer examples of different kinds of policies and practices along the continuum. Sitting with each group, a trainer helps draw out the analysis and makes suggestions about how change could happen. By the end of the three-day training, this process of analyzing structural racism within their institutions will help build a sense of coherence and unity within each team and serve as the basis for creating a twenty-year vision, a five-year goal statement, and two-year objectives that they can bring back to the church with them.

a spiritual journey to dismantle structural racism within their personal lives, institutions and communities.

Organizational Capacity

Crossroads Ministry has one national office in Chicago, IL and a regional office in Wisconsin. The program has approximately 10 core trainers and, over the past twelve years, has helped create more than 200 anti-racism teams in various U.S. institutions. The program's training model shares a common analysis of racism with the People's Institute and regularly brings in People's Institute trainers for specific portions of their training. Yet Crossroad's application of the analysis to a range of institutional settings is unique and has led to innovative analytical tools and a distinct team-based approach to institutional change. In addition to its three-phase team training process that takes place over the course of a year and develops the capacity for long-term institutional change, the organization offers a Leadership Training Institute to provide advanced training and training-of-trainers. Crossroads' analytical framework remains focused on racism rather than other forms of oppression and looks at the binary dynamics between whites and people of color, rather than varied relations between people of color.

Types of Participants

Crossroads offers trainings to a broad range of educational, religious and community-based institutions that are committed to community change and justice. Almost 70% of the program's work is with faith-based institutions such as churches and religious universities. Trainers commented that they rarely work with corporations because such organizations seem less concerned about the need to address institutional racism. Crossroads asks institutions that they work with to make a one-year commitment to a training that prepares them for long term organizing work. The program views transformation and leadership of institutions, especially religious and community-based institutions, as

an important and often neglected component of building a multi-cultural, anti-racist movement in the U.S.

UNDERSTANDING & INTERVENING AGAINST RACISM

Understanding the Problem

Crossroads Ministry brings a strong spiritual understanding to the analysis of structural racism and explicitly focuses on the moral imperative of anti-racism work in institutions. Like the People's Institute, Crossroads understands racism as the combination of race prejudice and the misuse of power in institutions and social systems. Institutional support of white privilege and power holds racism in place and perpetuates the oppression of people of color.

The program examines both different historical periods that created a tradition of institutional racism, as well as struggles against such injustices. For example, they categorize historic oppression into four distinct eras including: 1) the first three hundred fifty years of American history of colonization, genocide, slavery, expansion/annexation and the severe devaluation of labor; 2) the next one hundred years of Jim Crow laws, segregation, reservations, neo-colonialism and internment camps; 3) twenty years of civil rights, Native American and farm workers' social change movements; and 4) thirty years of post-civil rights racism.

The training model also looks at the misuses of power including racism's oppression of people of color and preservation of white power and privilege. The model examines the reciprocal relationship between white privilege and the oppression of people of color and also reviews the socialization and internalization of superiority and inferiority. Finally, trainings focus on the dynamics of cultural and institutional racism that destroy, distort, discount and discredit non-dominant cultures.

Crossroads critiques many diversity programs that work with institutions suggesting that they tend to change only the most visible or superficial aspects of institutions such as programs and personnel. Trainers commented that such programs only result in making white-controlled institutions more colorful. Crossroads' model suggests that programs that focus on improving relationships between personnel but affect no structural or cultural change in an institution actually reinforce existing racist norms and structures.

Addressing the Problem

Crossroads' training model suggests that the best way to address these problems is to develop a commitment to long-term, systemic transformation in institutions that is led internally and connected externally to the community. The program uses a team-based approach where participants are equipped to plan, implement and evaluate strategies that lead their institutions toward racial equity and justice.

Crossroads' model involves three phases that build upon each other over the course of twelve to eighteen months. The first phase requires institutions to form a planning and design task force that is responsible for: 1) creating an anti-racism project description including a statement of purpose, a timeline, and a budget; 2) developing a plan for recruitment and selection of the institution's anti-racism team; 3) gaining a commitment from the institution's leadership to conduct the anti-racism work, including an accountability and evaluation plan; 4) securing funding for the team training process; and 5) selecting the anti-racism team for the institution.

The second phase includes a three-day training that focuses on teambuilding for the anti-racist team, educating the team in a common framework for understanding individual, cultural and institutional racism, and developing team coherence based on an analysis of racism within their institution. The second phase also includes an extended period for implementing their institutional analysis and preliminary action plans.

The third phase of Crossroads' model offers a five-day intensive training that focuses on developing anti-racist skills and strategies. Institutional teams outline a twenty-year vision, five-year goals, and two-year objectives for anti-racism work within their institution. Crossroads provides training and coaching in developing team members' teaching skills so that teams can conduct educational events within their institution on the nature of institutional racism and the need for change. Trainers also provide organizing skills to enable team members to design, implement and evaluate structural change efforts within their institutions.

Training Methods

Crossroads' training model is consistent across groups, though institutional teams are required to adapt and apply their new understanding to their institutional context. Trainings are clearly structured and the dominant lecture format is supplemented with other learning tools such as question and answer sessions, small group exercises, analysis of videos, and journaling. The structured nature of the training minimizes self-disclosure in large group discussions, but leaves room for sharing personal experiences during small-group and paired discussions. Trainers often integrate participants' core values or religious beliefs into their program. Participants receive a packet of training materials during each session and a variety of relevant books, videotapes and music CDs are available through the program.

The program's three phases and team trainings within each phase build upon each other.[6] The first session focuses on defining structural

> *"You can make an institution act differently by community organizing, but you can't change the inner life of the institution that way. Making an institution's identity, mindset or ideology anti-racist is more of an inside job."*

---

6. The researchers were only able to attend the first-phase training and base their analysis and summary on this limited experience.

racism and analyzing the historical development and institutional manifestations of racial oppression. Initial exercises trace the history of racism and resistance to racism in the U.S. Trainers also review a series of definitions for understanding race prejudice, power, and individual, cultural and institutional racism. Teams discuss the discomfort and difficulty in exploring attitudes, feelings and theories about race, and participants are given opportunities to journal some of their experiences. The program uses movies, news documentaries and group caucusing to spark reflection on white privilege, the socialization of racial oppression, and the internalization of racial superiority and inferiority. Trainers discuss blocks to united anti-racist organizing and focus on tools and strategies for dismantling racism. Finally, teams are asked to apply their new analytical framework for racism to their respective institutions.

Additional training sessions in phase two and three focus on designing, implementing and evaluating a strategy for long-term, anti-racist change within each team's specific institution. They also include significant opportunities for reflection on the actions taken between training sessions.

THEORY OF CHANGE

Crossroads' model holds that dismantling racism requires institutions that negatively impact communities of color and perpetuate poverty to become accountable to the communities they serve. Because institutional systems are particularly resistant to change, anti-racist transformation must be led by teams inside the institution and sanctioned by a commitment from institutional leadership. Identifying and changing fundamental policies, structures and mission—the deeper levels of institutional identity and purpose—is critical to successful institutional change.

> *"An institution with structured anti-racism policies will not tolerate racist attitudes and behavior. They will hire people and say, 'the first qualification for this job is that you have to get anti-racism training.' When the system demands that, its not just an individual's choice."*

The program emphasizes the interdependence of community organizing and institutional transformation, and suggests that an institution cannot work for change isolated from the communities it serves. At the same time, community change does not always result in institutional transformation. Trainers suggest that a transformed institution is evidenced by its participation in changing the larger society.

DISTINGUISHING FEATURES

Like its sister organization, the People's Institute, Crossroads provides a much needed analysis of institutional and structural forms of racism. The program's three-phase, team-based training model is unique in its focus on long-term, core transformation within specific institutions. Crossroad's Leadership Development Institute further equips institutional teams to conduct ongoing, internal, anti-racism work independent of Crossroads. The program encourages institutions to develop their own internal capacity and methodology for change and connect these to community anti-racism movements. The model provides an important complement and alternative to more typical diversity or multicultural training programs that focus primarily on individual or intergroup dimensions of racism.

Crossroads' integration of faith and spiritual dimensions of anti-racism work with the institutional analysis makes it particularly well suited for work in a variety of religious institutions and organizations. The program's commitment to building a multicultural, anti-racist social movement within institutions across the U.S. also makes the lessons of the team-based model that has evolved over the past twelve years applicable to a wide variety of community-based and social service institutions and organizations.

CROSSROADS MINISTRY

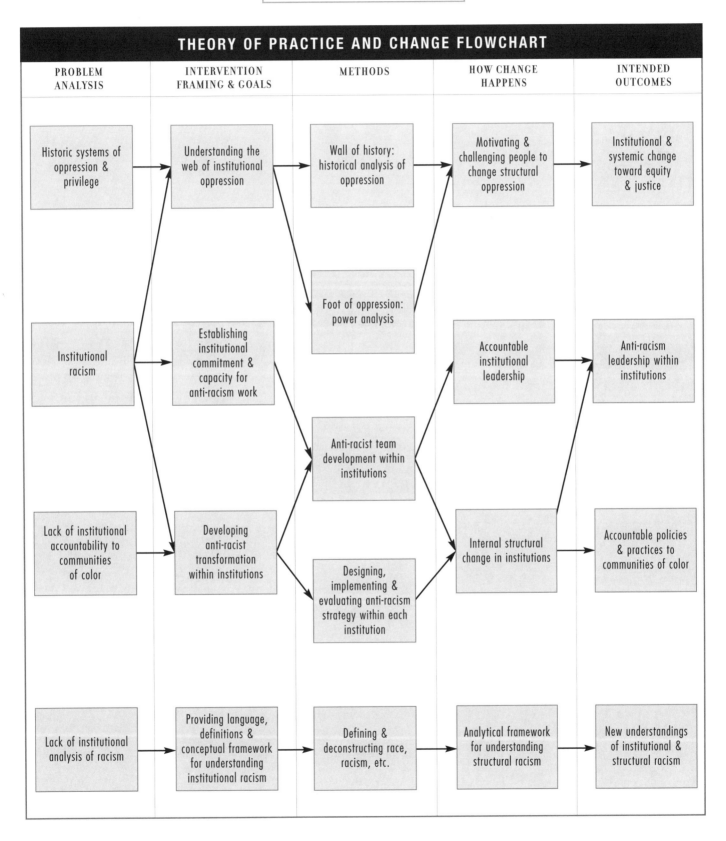

THEORY OF PRACTICE AND CHANGE FLOWCHART

PROBLEM ANALYSIS	INTERVENTION FRAMING & GOALS	METHODS	HOW CHANGE HAPPENS	INTENDED OUTCOMES
Historic systems of oppression & privilege	Understanding the web of institutional oppression	Wall of history: historical analysis of oppression	Motivating & challenging people to change structural oppression	Institutional & systemic change toward equity & justice
		Foot of oppression: power analysis		
Institutional racism	Establishing institutional commitment & capacity for anti-racism work	Anti-racist team development within institutions	Accountable institutional leadership	Anti-racism leadership within institutions
Lack of institutional accountability to communities of color	Developing anti-racist transformation within institutions	Designing, implementing & evaluating anti-racism strategy within each institution	Internal structural change in institutions	Accountable policies & practices to communities of color
Lack of institutional analysis of racism	Providing language, definitions & conceptual framework for understanding institutional racism	Defining & deconstructing race, racism, etc.	Analytical framework for understanding structural racism	New understandings of institutional & structural racism

Study Circles Resource Center

> "... *if you get people from many*
>
> *different backgrounds and viewpoints*
>
> *together and give them a process*
>
> *for talking things out,*
>
> *you can find common ground,*
>
> *and make community change based*
>
> *on that common ground.*"

STUDY CIRCLES RESEARCH CENTER

SUMMARY INFORMATION

ORGANIZATIONAL FOCUS	**Problem:** Race relations, racism, separation, lack of interaction, distrust. **Solution:** Dialogue, deliberative democracy, citizen participation, inclusion, civic engagement, civil society.
ORGANIZATIONAL HISTORY & CONTEXT	Founded in 1989 by the Topsfield Foundation. Rooted in U.S. citizen assemblies such as town meetings. Mission: "...to advance deliberative democracy and improve the quality of life in the U.S."
THEORY OF PRACTICE	Democracy Building.
ORGANIZATIONAL CAPACITY	One national office. Dialogue guides and discussion materials available free and on-line.
SERVICES	Facilitator training and ongoing technical assistance; organizing training, technical assistance and implementation consultation when requested.
TYPES OF PARTICIPANTS	Large number of people who represent the diversity of backgrounds, viewpoints and experiences in the community. Organized by coalitions of local or national organizations. Sanctioned and supported by official leaders.
LEVEL OF ANALYSIS	Individual, Intergroup and Structural.
PROBLEM ANALYSIS	Racism and tensions in race relations come from separation, division and distrust among racial, ethnic and cultural groups, lack of forums and skills for dialogue and difficulty talking about racial issues.
INTERVENTION PRINCIPLES	Improving race relations and fighting racism requires bringing people together to explore diverse perspectives on racial issues, identifying common ground, building cooperative relationships and developing individual and joint action steps for making community change.
INTERVENTION METHODS	Build coalitions to develop community-wide Study Circle action forums. Standard dialogue model for all groups that can be adapted by participants. Ten to Fifteen participants meet for five sessions over a period of weeks or months. Clear and detailed materials and dialogue guides. Dialogue about personal experiences, divergent viewpoints and public polices as primary learning methods.
INTENDED OUTCOMES	Change attitudes. Promote deeper understanding of racism and race relations. Build cooperative relationships, identify action steps. Change community decision-making processes. Community-wide meetings for action and change.
THEORY OF CHANGE	Interpersonal and intergroup contact. Sharing personal stories and experiences. Finding common ground and building trusting, cooperative relationships. A critical mass of individuals and citizen coalitions create structural change.
CONTACT INFORMATION	Director: Martha McCoy P.O. Box 203, Pomfret, CT 06258 phone: 860-928-2616 email: scrc@neca.com www.studycircles.org

Mission & History

Established in 1989 as a project of the Topsfield Foundation, the Study Circles Resource Center (Study Circles) is a non-profit, non-partisan organization "...dedicated to advancing deliberative democracy and improving the quality of life in the U.S." Study Circles has built its national reputation on developing a community-based dialogue model, providing training and consulting to national and local organizations that implement the model, and distributing clear and detailed, practical publications on citizen dialogue and action about a variety of public issues.

The Study Circles model traces its roots to early U.S. civic traditions that fostered participatory, small-group discussions of important public issues such as town meetings. Like these citizen assemblies, the dialogue model offers community members and leaders an opportunity to get to know each other, consider different points of view, explore disagreements and discover common ground. Through an open dialogue that recognizes the complexity of racism and race relations in the U.S., participants can begin to better understand the problem and each other, and build cooperative relationships to make change in their communities. Diverse coalitions of organizations can establish community-wide dialogues that foster large-scale action and change.

Although this summary focuses specifically on their racism and race relations work, Study Circles offers dialogue resources on a variety of public issues such as crime and violence, education and youth issues,

---

SETTING THE SCENE

"I REALLY don't think we need any new laws based on race," suggests Leslie, a white middle-age teacher at a local high school. "The civil rights movement did a good job passing anti-discrimination legislation. No, the problem now is that our institutions are not enforcing them well. If anything, we should improve that. And I think we need more policies that will help create jobs and economic opportunities in our inner cities, without regard to color." Leslie looks at each of the other eleven northern Virginian residents who are attending this fourth meeting of a Study Circle on racism, inviting their response. The discussion has become animated, yet friendly, as participants talk about different policy needs for their community that would help improve local race relations.

"Of course you think that," John, an African American minister from a nearby church, comments with a teasing smile, "but our government still hasn't acknowledged all of the wrongs done to people of color in this country, and this history is the source of racial inequity today. A few anti-discrimination laws aren't going to solve that. Public apologies,

reparations, and a review of *all* our policies to eliminate their racist assumptions are needed if we really want to fight racism." The group is silent a moment, acknowledging the difference of opinion between Leslie and John. It might have been the beginning of a shouting match or the end of the discussion just a few weeks earlier when this group first started meeting. But John and Leslie know each other better now. John has even given a presentation to one of Leslie's classes and they often joke before meetings about their different views.

Like most Study Circles groups, these 11 participants have spent the last few meetings exploring their different ideas about racism and race relations and developed a respect for each other and in some cases a friendship along the way. The facilitator has helped participants identify many of their shared concerns and common interests. While some were ready to start planning cooperative projects in the community from the start, all participants now recognize that the dialogue has deepened their understanding of the issues, increased their trust and appreciation of other group members, and provided a solid basis for work together in the future.

police-community relations, achievement gap, and community growth and development. The program fits clearly within the democracy building theory of practice.

Organizational Capacity

Hundreds of communities and cities across the U.S. have conducted dialogues using the Study Circles model. The program's clear and detailed guides support the development of peer facilitators rather than professional or "expert" facilitators. This has been an important ingredient in the growth and expansion of these dialogue efforts. Study Circles' resources on racism and race relations are available free at their website and at minimal cost by mail to communities across the country and include publications such as: *Facing the Challenge of Racism and Race Relations: Democratic Dialogue and Action for Stronger Communities; Toward a More Perfect Union in an Age of Diversity; Focus on Study Circles Newsletter; Organizing Community-Wide Dialogue for Action Change; and Facilitator Training Guide.*

Types of Participants

The coalitions of diverse programs that organize Study Circles try to attract a cross-section of community members to the dialogue process and often make a special effort to include people who are resistant or reluctant to talk about racial issues. In addition, Study Circles invite support or endorsement from top-level, local officials such as the Mayor's office or City Council to enhance the credibility of the dialogue, provide incentive for community participation and facilitate action.

National and local organizations such as the YMCA, city human relations commissions and church groups, often form local coalitions to organize community-wide Study Circles and tend to draw participants from their broad base of constituents. The dialogues are designed to bring together people from diverse backgrounds, with the understanding that multi-racial groups provide representation of different perspectives and experiences, create buy-in from a variety of stakeholders in the community, and offer the potential for more innovative solutions and effective action.

The Study Circles program is based on the premise that diversity is an essential part of democratic life and that inclusion and equality of different identity groups is a critical ingredient of healthy communities. At the same time, the program has designed resource guides that focus specifically on race relations and racism as a separate topic, recognizing that these issues are complex enough to be discussed in their own right, without the additional layers of other group identities such as gender, age and religion.

UNDERSTANDING & INTERVENING IN RACISM & RACE RELATIONS

Understanding the Problem

Unlike many training programs that provide specific understandings or definitions about racism, Study Circles stresses the importance of working with the ideas and assumptions that participants bring to the dialogue. Nevertheless, a number of assumptions about causes of racial tensions are inherent in their model, including: separation and division among racial, ethnic and cultural groups; difficulty talking about racism; lack of public forums and skills for discussing public issues; and lack of community-wide networks for action and change.

Study Circles draws attention to the geographic, economic, social and political separation among racial groups and suggests that misperceptions, stereotypes, fear and distrust have grown within this separation that prevent people from working together on common concerns. In addition, communities often lack forums for bringing people together to discuss public issues and where opportunities exist, people often fall into habits of argumentation and debate rather than constructive dialogue. The program also highlights the difficulty of talking about race and racism: Issues often seem too big or overwhelming, stir up strong emotions, and touch on issues of power and privilege that can be uncomfortable. Even when everyone seems to care about the issues, the language used to discuss them creates confusion and conflict, community members do not necessarily trust each other, and people do not even agree on what the issues are.

Addressing the Problem

Study Circles suggests that the best way to address these problems is to provide a forum that brings people together to explore diverse perspectives on racism and race relations, find common ground, develop cooperative relationships, and identify action steps for making community change. The program is founded on the principle that progress on race relations can only occur when all stakeholders are included in defining the problems and finding ways to work together to solve them. The model recognizes the unique manifestations of racism for different groups and in different U.S. regions, and it explores the divergent perspectives represented in the very language used to discuss issues of racism and race relations. Strategic action for addressing community racism is based upon common understandings, cooperative relationships that are established through dialogue, and community-wide action planning forums.

> *"Once people know each other on a personal level and become part of each others' stories, they can better see their own biases and can make real connections with each other."*

Dialogue Methods

Community-wide Study Circles are typically organized by a diverse coalition of programs that reflect the whole community. Drawing on its broad base of constituents, this coalition brings together large numbers of community members from all walks of life to participate in multiple circles, or small dialogue groups, across the community.

Each of the Study Circles typically involves 10-15 community participants meeting for five or more sessions over a series of weeks or months. All dialogues are facilitated and seek to establish a safe and blame-free environment for exploration of issues. Facilitators suggest that Study Circles are usually initiated when communities feel that they are "stuck" or divided around an issue or upcoming policy decision; there is an ongoing problem that is eroding the well-being of the community; or communities experience a crisis that divides racial groups.

The dialogue structure generally moves from the personal to the political, stressing the importance of engaging participants in personal, relational and structural change. The first and second sessions focus on participants' personal beliefs about and experiences with racism, and an analysis of different perspectives about the nature of the problem. The third, fourth and fifth sessions explore options for solving the identified problems, examine past and potential community policies, and develop individual and joint actions plans for addressing racism locally and nationally. Community-wide study circles often result in an action forum that brings together all of circles to work together on the action ideas that came out of the dialogues and organize coordinated strategies for community change.

Study Circles Resource Center provides guides for facilitators and participants that have clear and detailed information about organizing and facilitating the dialogue, discussion questions and exercises for each session, tips for moving from talk to action, methods of adapting the model to different situations, a comparison of dialogue and debate processes, and a bibliography on racism and race relations in the U.S.

THEORY OF CHANGE

The model suggests that exploring different viewpoints and sharing experiences of racism facilitate individual attitudes and behavior change. New, trusting, intergroup relationships are also built through these positive, small-group interactions. Organizing community-wide action forums helps translate new understandings and relationships into specific action strategies. The program suggests that the new understandings and relationships gained in dialogue provide the basis for structural change, however, facilitators stress that dialogues are not a quick-fix solution, but rather a first step in a longer process of community transformation.

> *"After hearing a particular individual tell her story, you're not indifferent or disengaged, or at a distance. It's an actual person that you know, who's dealing with something. That changes how you behave."*

DISTINGUISHING FEATURES

Because Study Circles dialogues explore public issues and challenge current practices while maintaining allegiance to the basic principles of democratic deliberation, discourse and action, the model is attractive and acceptable to a broad range of individuals and groups in the U.S. Study Circles dialogues are particularly useful in providing more sophisticated understandings of the issues and problems and developing well-thought out, consensus-based decisions for long-term change. In addition, the open and participatory nature of the model engages and empowers participants, builds new cooperative partnerships, and enhances community buy-in for social change initiatives. Study Circles' model offers particularly clear and detailed materials that foster multi-faceted understanding of these complex issues and allow for easy replication of the model in different communities throughout the country. Finally, the community-wide model effectively integrates individual, intergroup and structural dimensions of change toward racial equity and inclusion.

THEORY OF PRACTICE AND CHANGE FLOWCHART

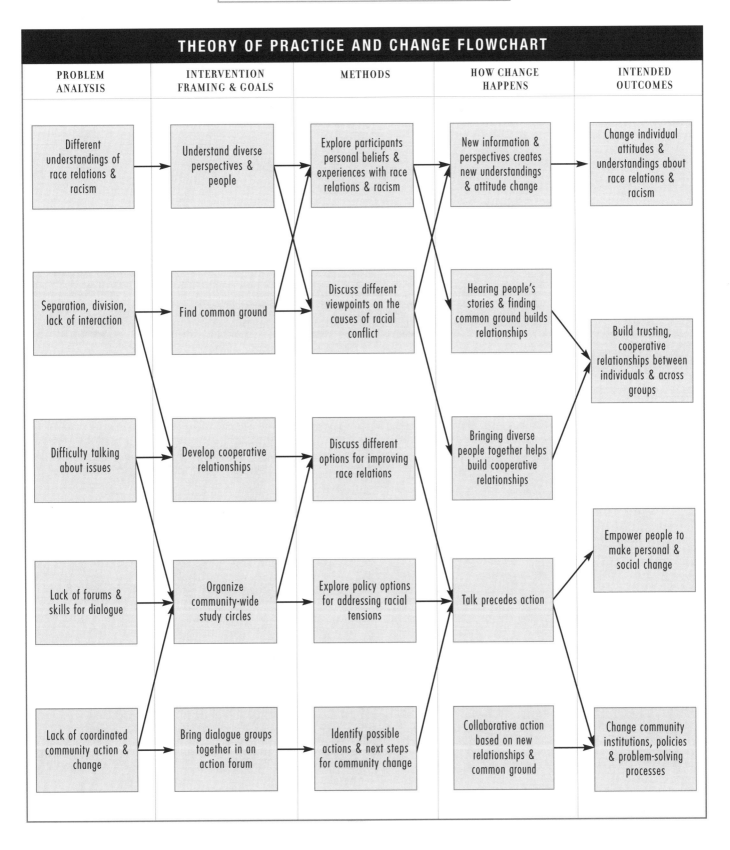

PROBLEM ANALYSIS	INTERVENTION FRAMING & GOALS	METHODS	HOW CHANGE HAPPENS	INTENDED OUTCOMES
Different understandings of race relations & racism	Understand diverse perspectives & people	Explore participants personal beliefs & experiences with race relations & racism	New information & perspectives creates new understandings & attitude change	Change individual attitudes & understandings about race relations & racism
Separation, division, lack of interaction	Find common ground	Discuss different viewpoints on the causes of racial conflict	Hearing people's stories & finding common ground builds relationships	Build trusting, cooperative relationships between individuals & across groups
Difficulty talking about issues	Develop cooperative relationships	Discuss different options for improving race relations	Bringing diverse people together helps build cooperative relationships	
Lack of forums & skills for dialogue	Organize community-wide study circles	Explore policy options for addressing racial tensions	Talk precedes action	Empower people to make personal & social change
Lack of coordinated community action & change	Bring dialogue groups together in an action forum	Identify possible actions & next steps for community change	Collaborative action based on new relationships & common ground	Change community institutions, policies & problem-solving processes

HOPE IN THE CITIES

*"We are seeking
to change the world
first by being willing
to change ourselves."*

HOPE IN THE CITIES

SUMMARY INFORMATION

ORGANIZATIONAL FOCUS	**Problem:** Racism, historic injustices and oppression, group victimization, white fear. **Solution:** Racial reconciliation, healing, honest conversation, acknowledgment, repentance, forgiveness, responsibility.
ORGANIZATIONAL HISTORY & CONTEXT	Founded in 1990 in Richmond, VA as a Moral Re-armament (MRA) program. Roots in multi-faith religious traditions, MRA philosophy and group psychodynamic theory. Mission: "…to create just and inclusive communities through reconciliation among racial, ethnic and religious groups based on personal and institutional transformation."
THEORY OF PRACTICE	Healing and Reconciliation.
ORGANIZATIONAL CAPACITY	One national office in Richmond, VA. Four to five core trainers and staff. Additional consultants and facilitators. A variety of publications, videos and other resource materials available.
SERVICES	Weekend dialogue on Race, Economics and Jurisdiction. Racial Reconciliation dialogue programs in twelve U.S. cities and available nationwide. Racial reconciliation events and conferences. Ongoing facilitator training and consultation when requested.
TYPES OF PARTICIPANTS	Cross-section of community organizations, citizens and local political or civic leaders. Specific groups (e.g., Jews and blacks; Sons of Confederate Veterans and blacks).
LEVEL OF ANALYSIS	Individual, Intergroup and Structural.
PROBLEM ANALYSIS	Unacknowledged historical injustices and group victimization have given rise to a culture of blame, guilt and denial around racial issues, which undermine attempts to meet community needs.
INTERVENTION PRINCIPLES	Racial healing and reconciliation come from hearing and acknowledging historic racial injustices and human traumas, recognizing common humanity between groups, repenting and atoning for past wrong doings, forgiving and receiving forgiveness, and taking personal responsibility for creating a better future.
INTERVENTION METHODS	Standard dialogue model for all groups that is flexible depending on group dynamics. Presentation, dialogue and experiential exercises as primary learning tools. Public events to enable communities to acknowledge painful history. Clear, detailed and systematic materials and manuals.
INTENDED OUTCOMES	Promote understanding of historic and current injustices experienced by African Americans and other people of color. Acknowledge unhealed wounds of white Americans. Personal transformation. Promote acknowledgement, repentance and forgiveness between groups. Racial healing and reconciliation among participants. Move all parties beyond the historical legacy of victimhood and guilt to become partners for community change.
THEORY OF CHANGE	Sharing groups' experiences of oppression. New information, personal reflection and vulnerability to emotions leads to individual transformation. Rituals and symbols foster large group and social change. Recognizing common humanity helps build relationships across groups. Resilient relationships create social change.
CONTACT INFORMATION	National Director: Robert Corcoran; Associate National Director: Paige Chargois 1103 Sunset Avenue, Richmond, VA Phone: 804-358-1764 email: hopecities@aol.com

Mission & History

Founded in 1990 as a Moral Re-Armament (MRA) initiative—now known as Initiatives of Change—Hope in the Cities is a non-profit, inter-racial, multi-faith program with a mission to "...set in motion a process of healing through honest conversation on race, reconciliation and responsibility." The program initially focused on race relations in communities of Richmond, VA, but now organizes and sponsors dialogues, training, conferences, public forums and events to address racial conflicts and promote healing and reconciliation in cities and communities nationwide.

Hope in the Cities' approach reflects the philosophical roots of Initiatives of Change (formerly MRA) and is grounded in multi-faith traditions that emphasize the moral and spiritual imperative of peace and racial reconciliation. One of the underlying tenets of the program is that personal experience and transformation is the foundation for social change. The program emphasizes experience rather than doctrine and encourages individuals to find their unique contribution to the social, economic, political and moral changes needed in the world. Through a spirit of hope and selflessness, the Hope in the Cities program seeks to heal the wounds of history, encourage care and responsibility in social relationships, and build networks among people from different faiths and cultures who are committed to work for reconciliation, justice and peace.

Organizational Capacity

Hope in the Cities has one national office in Richmond, VA with a full-time staff of 4-5 individuals. The program works closely with a wide variety of experienced, independent facilitators and practitioners who share a similar philosophical approach to their racial reconciliation work.

SETTING THE SCENE

ON A BRIGHT Sunday morning in early spring, 25 local participants representing a broad spectrum of communities in Richmond, VA are meeting for the final day of Hope in the Cities' weekend Dialogue on Race, Economics and Jurisdiction. Gathered in five small working groups, participants are completing a timeline on chart paper that covers the length of the large meeting room wall. Each group works on one decade, from the 1950s through the 1990s, recalling both the cultural and political changes that have impacted their local communities.

Participants are excited as they reminisce about cultural landmarks of the time, such as the best restaurants, shopping malls, high schools, places to live, dance spots, etc. They also spend time remembering the public policies or major government, economic or community development initiatives such as desegregation, jurisdictional changes and new highway funds that helped shape their community each decade. The room is at times loud with laughter and silent with outrage as participants recall and record these memories together. Within an hour the wall chart is covered in a collage of brightly colored words containing the collective memory of community change in Richmond. Participants go back to their seats exhausted, remarking with both pride and regret as they look through the different decades.

"Let's look at some of these public policy initiatives," suggests one of the facilitators. "What was their intent? What was their impact?"

A conversation begins about some of the housing initiatives from the fifties that were intended to provide low-income housing, but ended up creating concentrations of poverty. Another discussion follows about the community college initiatives designed to broaden the educational base and encourage technical training, but also creating segregation in education. Finally, they discuss desegregation and integration initiatives that were intended to promote social equity and justice, but also resulted in decimating the black economic base, encouraging white flight, and fueling massive inter-racial mistrust and white resistance to integration.

"Policy initiatives developed in good faith, with good intentions, created negative impacts," summarizes one of the facilitators. "We need to recognize both intention and impact in looking at our histories...We need deep and transforming healing between the races, because the division of history and decades of inequity feed today's policy debates and public programs."

The review of social policies and collective histories from multiple perspectives is one of the defining characteristics of this and other Hope in the Cities dialogues. Like many other exercises over the weekend, this historical analysis of the community helps lay a strong foundation for individual transformation and racial healing and reconciliation.

Hope in the Cities offers an intensive weekend dialogue model focused on community issues around race, economics and jurisdiction and a six-week dialogue model for racial reconciliation. In addition, the program is known for its 1993 "Richmond Unity Walk" where people from over 50 cities and 20 countries literally took a 'walk through history' in Richmond to acknowledge and mark significant sites in the painful history of racial oppression in the city. That walk, which was the centerpiece of their "Healing the Heart of America" conference, has been replicated in cities across the U.S.

Types of Participants

Hope in the Cities works with a broad range of community organizations, citizens and local political or civic leaders. Facilitators note that support from top, local leaders helps legitimize the dialogues, attract participants and implement action plans that result from the dialogues. Hope in the Cities' model works with multi-racial groups and focuses primarily on the black-white dimensions of racism. Though it has been adapted for use in regions where racial tensions are between different groups, the program suggests that relationships between blacks and whites are key to improving race relations in the U.S. The program also occasionally organizes dialogues on race relations for specific groups such as men, religious leaders, or Jews and blacks only.

UNDERSTANDING & INTERVENING AGAINST RACISM

Understanding the Problem

Hope in the Cities has a number of clearly articulated assumptions about the causes of racial tension and conflict. First, the program suggests that unacknowledged historic injustices against African Americans and other people of color in the U.S. have left enduring personal and public legacies. It also recognizes that the continued sense of pain and loss among white southerners and resentment towards northerners who have "forgotten" their own history of racism is a continued source of division. The program holds that when one group has been traumatized by oppression, the whole society—including both the victim and offender groups—is damaged. Because these wounds and losses have not been adequately acknowledged or atoned for, they do not heal.

The program also emphasizes the schism between the ideals of freedom and equality that the U.S. was founded on, and the legacies of bigotry and institutional oppression present in the U.S. For example, facilitators discuss Richmond's history as both a powerful home to visionary political leadership and a major center for slave trading, Jim Crow laws, and resistance to desegregation. The program focuses on racism, but also examines how cross-cutting issues such as class and geographic separation have impacted both individual and institutional dimensions of racial oppression.

Hope in the Cities suggests that another primary cause of current racial tensions is a tremendous fear among white people of saying or doing the wrong thing regarding race. Facilitators describe the culture of polite silence that has grown up out of this fear. The program holds that fear of being blamed, attacked, or feeling ignorant prevents white people from truly listening to others, taking responsibility for addressing past and current injustices, and taking the risks necessary to reconcile relationships.

Addressing the Problem

Hope in the Cities addresses these problems through a model based on three operating principles: 1) sustaining genuinely open dialogue that engages all sectors of the community; 2) public acts of acknowledgment and healing of specific racial history; and 3) acceptance of personal responsibility by each participant in the process of change. The program engages people representing a wide spectrum of political beliefs and social backgrounds. Hope in the Cities believes that everyone has something to bring to the table and that everyone has something to learn. Racial reconciliation is driven by a recognition of the common underlying humanity between divided groups, an acknowledgement of past wrongs, and the development of healing interracial relationships. The program suggests that people must hold themselves, their communities and their institutions accountable for needed change. It aims to move beyond the victim-victimizer paradigm to one of shared responsibility for community change.

Hope in the Cities' dialogues are designed to create a space for honest and healing conversations that rehumanize 'the other' and acknowledge people's losses and privileges. In keeping with the spiritual basis of its work, Hope in the Cities focuses on exploring shared core values among participants and a common humanity transcending identity group divisions.

The process of acknowledging injustices and another groups' suffering, repenting for such actions, giving and accepting forgiveness for past wrong doings, and taking responsibility for making change in the future is at the heart of Hope in the Cities' theory of practice and change. The program suggests that a slow and thoughtful historical review of groups' relationships can help surface important group traumas and injustices, and begin the process of healing. Acknowledgement and forgiveness help release, on a deeper level, resistance to completing the mourning process and moving forward into problem-solving and action-planning for a better future.

The program suggests that a pre-condition for the processes of acknowledgement, repentance

"I think we've always felt that, in essence, the program deals with the moral and spiritual issues of race. As far as we're concerned, we have to deal with it at that level. It's not going to be resolved purely by legislation or by an analysis of the issues. It's important to understand the problem, but even once we've understood it, it doesn't necessarily solve it."

and forgiveness is a safe environment where people will stretch their thinking and understanding beyond what is familiar, and build relationships outside their usual comfort zone. Facilitators suggest that part of this stretching is asking participants to go beyond intellectualizing the problem to dealing with the feelings that are inherent in racial healing and reconciliation work. In addition, Hope in the Cities suggests that their dialogue models are really an organic process of uncovering existing resources and potential within individuals and communities rather than imparting specific knowledge or taking predetermined actions.

Dialogue Methods

Hope in the Cities' dialogue programs are based on a standard model that is adapted for different geographic regions and participant groups. There are two distinct dialogue models: a six-session model on racial reconciliation and an intensive-weekend model on race, economics and jurisdiction. Both are very structured, providing interactive exercises and specific questions to focus and guide the conversation. Both are also based on similar principles and philosophy, and provide participants with clear manuals and materials. The distinction between the two models lies in their structure and focus. One model consists of six consecutive two-hour sessions and focuses more on personal reflection and actions related to race relations and racism in general; the other takes place over a two and a half day intensive weekend and focuses more on structural analysis of racism in a particular city or community and cross-cutting issues such as class and jurisdiction.[7] This brief description focuses on the weekend model of race, economics and jurisdiction.

---

7. Only the weekend dialogue was observed in this research, so descriptions and analysis are confined to that model.

The weekend dialogue usually begins with a two-hour presentation about the interrelated issues of race, class and jurisdiction in Richmond or the particular city where the model is offered. The presentation focuses on how racism is played out structurally in urban/suburban racial demographics, development, taxes, income, and allocation of district resources (e.g., for school budgets, transportation, housing, etc.) and a host of other areas. This presentation provides a common basis for further conversation about the current realities of racism and race relations.

To begin the dialogue, participants spend time identifying their own core values and discussing them in relation to other participants' values. This exercise sparks an extended conversation on shared values and common humanity beneath more apparent differences. It also gives participants a chance to become better acquainted with each other and identify common ground for building relationships.

A key exercise focuses on developing a timeline for cultural and public policy changes in the city over the past five decades. This collective 'walk through history' provides the basis for conversation about the disparity between intention and impact and allows individuals to talk about their groups' and community's traumas (see Setting the Scene). Other exercises include small group work to build trusting relationships, effective cross-sectoral partnerships and personal visions for an ideal community. Finally, participants dialogue about personal, political, social, economic and spiritual dimensions of racial healing and reconciliation work, and discuss ways to integrate these dimensions in creating collaborative change. The dialogue on race, class and

"…citizens have initiated honest conversations—between people of all backgrounds— on matters of race, reconciliation and responsibility. They have chosen to move beyond blame and guilt, beyond hatred and fear, deciding to face the past with courage and honesty. They are demonstrating that through honesty, a willingness to embrace each others' painful experiences, and with God's power to change us, the wounds of the past can be healed and our nation become one community."

jurisdiction addresses both personal and social dimensions of racial reconciliation and provides a structural analysis of race-based economics and politics grounded in local communities.

THEORY OF CHANGE

Hope in the Cities views personal transformation as the foundation for improved intergroup relations and structural change. Individual-level or personal change happens through a process of sharing stories of personal and collective traumas and experiencing the emotions of those stories. Processes of acknowledgement, repentance, forgiveness and responsibility are also a vehicle for personal and relational transformation. Personal transformation becomes the cornerstone for healing intergroup relationships. The program suggests that strong relationships and networks among participants within the dialogue, and with identified partners outside the group, facilitate structural-level community change. These resilient relationships create the basis for planning long-term, community-level change, and working toward that new vision of racial healing and justice.

DISTINGUISHING FEATURES

Hope in the Cities offers a unique dialogue model that recognizes important spiritual and symbolic dimensions of racial reconciliation work. This focus unites participants in a healing agenda that relinquishes blame and focuses on constructive social change. The focus on historic racial injustices, processes of acknowledgement and forgiveness, and current racial, economic and political issues merges the spiritual and psychological aspects of racial reconciliation with a grounding in community issues and structures. The program's well-articulated theory of practice integrates individual and societal transformation with spiritual principles that make it appealing to a wide range of participants from different racial and cultural traditions. In addition to dialogue, the identification, training and nurturing of leadership at all levels is a vital component of Hope in the Cities' work with individuals and institutions. The program works toward developing diverse, self-sustaining teams capable of engaging all sectors in the work of reconciliation and justice. The program model is also remarkable in linking local, national and international levels of reconciliation work, and applying understandings gained in international reconciliation efforts to communities within the U.S. Finally, the program offers a variety of insightful publications and resources for understanding the complex dynamics of racial healing and reconciliation.

HOPE IN THE CITIES

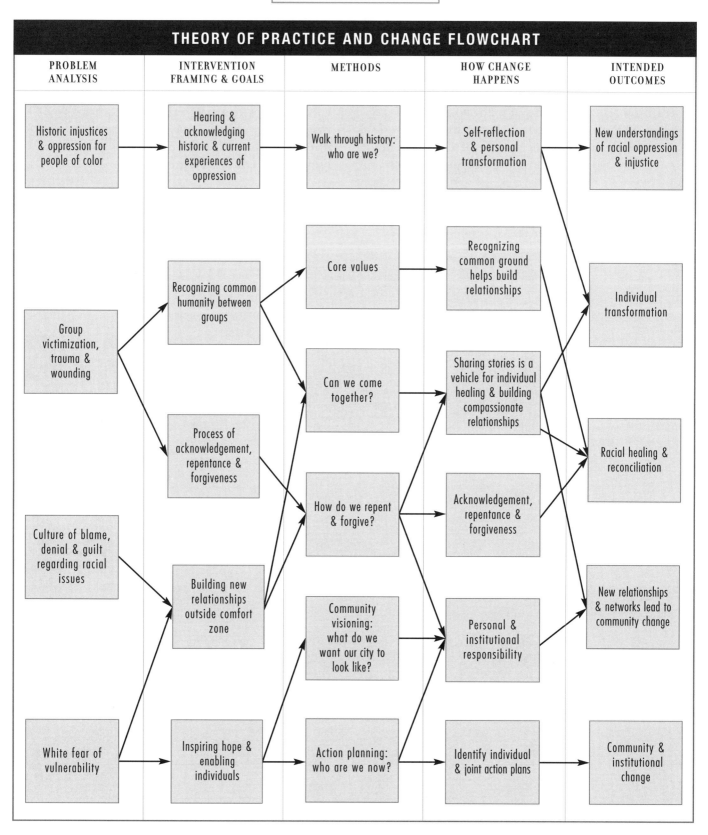

THEORY OF PRACTICE AND CHANGE FLOWCHART

PROBLEM ANALYSIS	INTERVENTION FRAMING & GOALS	METHODS	HOW CHANGE HAPPENS	INTENDED OUTCOMES
Historic injustices & oppression for people of color	Hearing & acknowledging historic & current experiences of oppression	Walk through history: who are we?	Self-reflection & personal transformation	New understandings of racial oppression & injustice
Group victimization, trauma & wounding	Recognizing common humanity between groups	Core values	Recognizing common ground helps build relationships	Individual transformation
	Process of acknowledgement, repentance & forgiveness	Can we come together?	Sharing stories is a vehicle for individual healing & building compassionate relationships	Racial healing & reconciliation
Culture of blame, denial & guilt regarding racial issues	Building new relationships outside comfort zone	How do we repent & forgive?	Acknowledgement, repentance & forgiveness	
		Community visioning: what do we want our city to look like?	Personal & institutional responsibility	New relationships & networks lead to community change
White fear of vulnerability	Inspiring hope & enabling individuals	Action planning: who are we now?	Identify individual & joint action plans	Community & institutional change

DISMANTLING RACISM INSTITUTE—
NATIONAL CONFERENCE FOR
COMMUNITY AND JUSTICE

"Our work is to transform

communities through

institutional change—

by empowering leaders—

so that all people will have

access to our nation's

opportunities and be

included in its promise."

DISMANTLING RACISM INSTITUTE—National Conference for Community & Justice

SUMMARY INFORMATION

ORGANIZATIONAL FOCUS	**Problem:** Racial oppression, racial polarization, white privilege, internalized racism. **Solution:** Dismantling racism, inclusive organizations, improved intergroup relations, personal awareness and responsibility, conflict resolution.
ORGANIZATIONAL HISTORY & CONTEXT	Founded in 1992 as an NCCJ program for the St. Louis region. Roots in human relations and social justice work. Mission: "create a critical mass of change agents in the St. Louis region who are skilled and motivated to intervene in oppressive situations, initiate programs and training, and offer support to each other with the long-term vision of dismantling racism in our region."
THEORY OF PRACTICE	Prejudice Reduction and Anti-Racism.
ORGANIZATIONAL CAPACITY	NCCJ has sixty-one offices across the U.S. in 34 States and the District of Columbia. Dismantling Racism (DR) Institute is a program of NCCJ in St. Louis, MO. Dismatling Racism Institute has six to eight trainers.
SERVICES	Six-day residential Dismantling Racism (DR) Institute and DR Institute for Educators. One-day Building Inclusive Community Workshop. Eight-day Anytown Youth Leadership Institute for high school youth. Dialogue Groups. Ongoing Dismantling Racism Network. Custom-designed training and consultation when requested.
TYPES OF PARTICIPANTS	Diverse racial, gender, age, professional background and level of leadership. Non-profit organizations, community groups, businesses and corporations, universities, government agencies, schools, youth organizations and religious institutions.
LEVEL OF ANALYSIS	Individual and Structural.
PROBLEM ANALYSIS	Racism is historically based and learned through a cycle of socialization where individuals are socially conditioned to collude in and perpetuate a process that systemically provides unequal access to opportunities, benefits and privileges. The legacy of oppression results in racial separation and polarization economically, politically, socially and geographically.
INTERVENTION PRINCIPLES	Dismantling racism requires education about racism and its impact on individuals and society; introspection and emotional awareness, which provides a personal foundation for dismantling racism; skills to address the challenges of racism; a network of allies committed to individual and institutional change; and action plans for building inclusive institutions and communities.
INTERVENTION METHODS	Standard, intensive model offered annually. Variety of learning tools including presentation, experiential exercises, discussion, journaling, caucusing, fishbowl, role-play, videos and skills training. Clear and detailed training manual and reader.
INTENDED OUTCOMES	Empowering individuals to be change agents in dismantling racism through education and introspection. Developing ongoing support networks to foster long-term systemic change. Changing structural policies and practices that perpetuate racism and racial polarization.
THEORY OF CHANGE	Change comes through a cycle of liberation that empowers individuals through introspection and education, empowers and motivates communities through alliances, and transforms institutions and communities through leadership and social action.
CONTACT INFORMATION	Program Director: Reggie Williams; Executive Director: Martin Rafanan 721 Olive, Suite 915, St. Louis, MO 63101 phone: 314-241-5103

Mission & History

The Dismantling Racism (DR) Institute was established in 1992 in St. Louis, MO, as a program of the National Conference for Community and Justice (NCCJ)[8] to "create a critical mass of change agents who are skilled and motivated to intervene in oppressive situations, initiate programs and training, and offer support to each other with the long-term vision of dismantling racism in our region." The program was originally created by Mary Webber, an activist and faith leader in St. Louis, as a diversity awareness and prejudice reduction program to address issues of racial polarization facing religious institutions in the region. It quickly expanded, however, to include a broad range of community and organizational leaders across the region and integrated a focus on structural and systemic aspects of racism. The six-day residential DR Institute now provides participants from the St. Louis region as well as other parts of the country with intensive training to increase understanding of racism's impact on individuals and society, and to build a network of change agents committed to individual, organizational and community change.

The DR program draws from both human relations and social justice perspectives in addressing racism. The training takes a participant-centered approach to learning and transformation, emphasizing the importance of individual change as a precursor and foundation for larger organizational and community change. The program stresses the importance of making the connection between

SETTING THE SCENE

AT A RURAL retreat center just outside of St. Louis, MO, 27 participants representing a cross-section of the diverse city are meeting for a six-day residential Dismantling Racism (DR) institute offered by the National Conference for Community and Justice (NCCJ). Now, toward the end of the third day of the intensive training, a feeling of community, comfort and respect permeates the group. All day, participants have been meeting, both in multi-racial groups and race-based caucuses, to explore issues of internalized oppression and white privilege.

They are now arranged for a fishbowl exercise to discuss how these issues effect their everyday lives. Women of color volunteer to be the first group to sit in the fishbowl, a small circle in the center of the larger group.

Trainers select the caucus of white men to be the first interviewers, and give them a short time to struggle together in agreeing on an 'interview question' for the women of color caucus. Finally, a representative from the white men's caucus asks the fishbowl group, "What is your impression of the perceived breakdown of family responsibility by young black males?"

Each of the women in the fishbowl takes a few minutes to respond to this question and the whole group is struck by the candor, honesty and variety of their answers. When they finish, participants from other caucuses comment on their perceptions of the women of color's answers and behavior. The trust in the room is evidenced by the respect, polite confrontation, and personal sincerity during this exchange. Soon it is time for another caucus to sit in the fishbowl and respond to a new interview question.

Like many of the learning tools used during this intense week of training, participants find this exercise to be a powerful vehicle for developing new awareness and understanding. It provides a window into the impact of racism on both individuals and social systems, and encourages participants to address obvious issues that "sit on the table" as well as to dig deeper to uncover those concealed "under the table." Finally, trainers use this and other exercises to foster the individual introspection and education that is the foundation of effective change agents, and to create networks of allies who can work together to bring about long-term, multi-level institutional and community change.

---

8. The National Conference for Community and Justice is a human relations organization founded in 1927 with a mission to "fight bias, bigotry and racism in America through education, advocacy and conflict resolution."

personal transformation and institutional change. The primary focus is on the "black/white" paradigm of race relations relevant to the local dynamics of St. Louis. The framework is also based upon the "tapestry of oppression"—a conceptual tool that underscores how complex social relations place all people, at one time or another, in positions of privilege or oppression based on age, gender, sexual orientation, ability, or educational achievement. The program integrates the prejudice reduction, diversity/multiculturalism and anti-racism theories of practice.

Organizational Capacity

Over the past ten years, more than 300 people have participated in the intensive, six-day DR program that is offered once a year in St. Louis. NCCJ–St. Louis has recently initiated a successful DR Institute specifically for educators and is organizing additional specialized Institutes for other sectors including: faith communities, government, economic leaders, media and advertising, and youth and emerging leaders. Other NCCJ offices in the Southern U.S. have begun to replicate the DR Institute trainings and the program model is considered one of NCCJ's most promising practices.

As part of the DR program, participants make an extended commitment to anti-racism work in their communities including: forty hours of community service over two years; follow-up coaching with NCCJ trainers to assess and improve participants' anti-racism efforts; ongoing participation in the DR support network of alumni; and supplemental trainings on a variety of topics. The DR program has a racially diverse core faculty of 6-8 trainers who are all graduates of the program and have considerable skills and experience in the areas of facilitation, counseling, organizational development, human rights advocacy, social work, education and social justice activism.

The DR program is part of NCCJ's larger CommUnity initiative designed to dismantle racist systems of attitudes, behaviors and institutional practices and foster racially inclusive organizations and communities in the St. Louis region. In addition to the six-day training, the CommUnity initiative includes: one-day "Building Inclusive Community" workshops; multi-session dialogue groups on race relations; "Anytown" youth leadership camps; and custom-designed training and consulting services.

Types of Participants

The DR Institute is designed for a diverse cross-section of St. Louis communities. Participants typically come from non-profit organizations, community groups, businesses and corporations, universities, government agencies, schools, youth organizations and religious institutions in the region. The program has an active participant outreach and selection process to ensure that all institute participants are both able and ready to make a commitment to anti-racism work and establish a group that is diverse in race, class, gender, age, professional background and level of leadership. During the program, participants have an opportunity to work in both multi-racial groups and in separate race-based caucuses.

While the majority of participants in the program are from the St. Louis region, the training is open to people from across the U.S. Participants from the St. Louis region become part of an ongoing support network. These local personal and professional relationships are crucial to making long-term, multi-level change in this concentrated geographic region. Participants from other parts of the U.S. are encouraged to find ways to replicate the program and develop anti-racist networks within their own communities.

UNDERSTANDING & INTERVENING AGAINST RACISM

Understanding the Problem

The DR Institute takes a multifaceted approach to understanding the causes of racism and racial polarization. Focused on the St. Louis region, the program examines the history of legal and institutional racial separation and oppression of African Americans, both locally and nationally, that creates current dynamics of racial segregation and polarization. The historical review also examines what was done to different communities of color for economic gain, what was taught that excused or covered up the mistreatment, how groups were characterized to justify their treatment, and how groups were dehumanized as means to an end.

The program also critically examines the cycle of socialization through which individuals become part of the racist system. The model explains that people are born into a society with racist systems in place and through no fault of their own are taught biases, stereotypes, misinformation, and racist social norms, values and practices. These are reinforced and sanctioned consciously and unconsciously through institutions (e.g., schools, media, religious institutions) and cultural practices (e.g., language, values, patterns of thought). By the time they reach adulthood, most people have internalized privilege or oppression based on their skin color and unknowingly collude in perpetuating a system that gives unequal access to opportunities and provides benefits and privileges to white people at the expense of people of color. Racism, like other forms of oppression, is a system of disadvantage and advantage.

The model recognizes that white privilege and internalized racism are two sides of the same coin, and that both the oppressors and the oppressed are complicit in perpetuating the racist system. In particular, the program suggests that people are part of the problem when they don't speak out against racism.

Addressing the Problem

To address these issues, the DR training model provides an intense emotional and introspective

> "During the Institute, people of different races get attached to each other and form relationships. It's hard to walk away from the realities of racism when it involves someone you care about."

program to help participants reflect upon their own experiences and beliefs about racism, develop a support network for ongoing dismantling racism work, and learn skills and processes for acting as change agents in their respective communities and institutions.

The training model suggests that breaking the cycle of socialization for racism requires that people participate in a cycle of liberation. Personal awareness, education and change are the first steps of the cycle. Seeking out new experiences and perspectives, and naming injustices and taking a personal stance further prepares individuals for changing how they value and interact with others. Building new relationships, support networks and coalitions within and between identity groups is the next step of the cycle, crucial for helping people take leadership roles in transforming their institutions and communities. Actions that dismantle structural and systemic racism help expand, inspire and support the circle of individuals who want to engage in this cycle of liberation and become social change agents.

The trainings are participant-centered, focusing on where individuals are in their personal journey, encouraging responsibility for dismantling racism without placing blame or guilt, and creating a safe space for taking the risks needed to make personal change. Work on internalized oppression and white privilege is a powerful component of the program and often triggers many of the emotional aspects of anti-racism work. The program also provides skills and processes for effective communication and feedback, conflict resolution, multicultural thinking, and action planning.

Training Methods

The six-day, residential structure of the DR Institute provides a uniquely intense experience for participants that builds strong, trusting relationships and allows for risk-taking that is essential for personal transformation. In addition, the extended duration allows for the use of a rich variety of learning tools such as presentation, experiential exercises, discussion, journaling, race-based caucusing, fishbowl, video, role-play and skills training. The training is designed to move from and connect the personal to the institutional levels of transformation. Participants receive a comprehensive training manual that includes detailed information about the program's concepts and exercises, and a variety of articles, bibliographies and informational resources for dismantling racism and other forms of oppression.

The initial portion of the training helps build trust among participants and develop a cohesive group. It also introduces skills for effective communication and feedback. The next portion of the training examines the history of oppression in the U.S., and the cycle of socialization and liberation, tying these into local community histories and participants' own experiences. Trainers also provide definitions and identify assumptions underlying their work.

Trainers then focus on racial identity development and address internalized oppression and white privilege. The program provides opportunities for learning and dialogue both in multi-racial groups and separate, race-based caucuses. Building upon this work, the training transitions into developing participants' skills as allies through work in 'Change Teams.' Participants learn additional skills for dismantling racism and resolving conflict through a series of role-plays and feedback called, "A day in the life of a change agent." The final portion of the training focuses on strategy development and action planning, addresses issues participants may face

"...to be effective in anti-racism work, you must have examined yourself and thought long and hard about where you are coming from."

as they re-enter their communities and organizations after the training, and helps participants plan next steps for work in with the DR network.

THEORY OF CHANGE

The DR Institute suggests that empowering individuals comes through education, introspection and developing anti-racist analysis and tools for change. There is an explicit understanding that participants must develop an understanding of how the issues of oppression impact them and begin a personal journey of transformation to be effective social change agents. Supported by personal and professional networks, alliances and coalitions, participants can take leadership roles in influencing community policies and practices and redefining the use of power. This process requires ongoing work and a broad network of support.

DISTINGUISHING FEATURES

The DR Institute provides a unique opportunity for individuals to begin their personal journey toward becoming social change agents. The intensity and community of the trainings facilitates in-depth personal change in participants and builds trusting, supportive relationships among them. Skilled and experienced trainers utilize a large variety of learning tools and training methods, to address a range of different individual and cultural learning styles. The program also provides an impressive binder of reading materials to address racism and other forms of oppression. The program's focus on the St. Louis region and new efforts within specific professional sectors such as education, makes it easier to provide ongoing personal and professional support for dismantling racism beyond the training period. Finally, the program has evolved over the past ten years based on participant feedback and provides an interesting model for replication in other regions.

THEORY OF PRACTICE AND CHANGE FLOWCHART

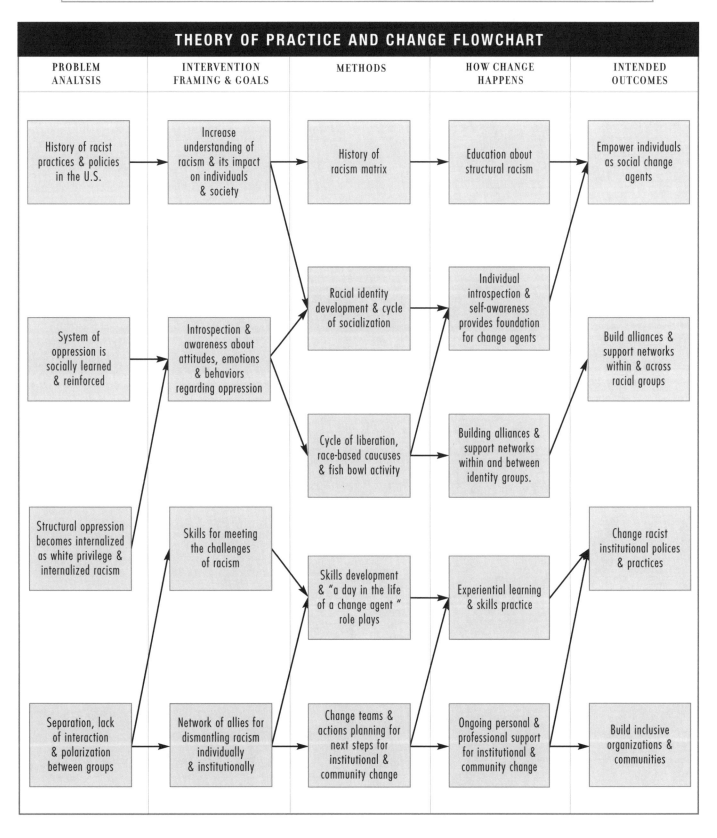

PROBLEM ANALYSIS	INTERVENTION FRAMING & GOALS	METHODS	HOW CHANGE HAPPENS	INTENDED OUTCOMES
History of racist practices & policies in the U.S.	Increase understanding of racism & its impact on individuals & society	History of racism matrix	Education about structural racism	Empower individuals as social change agents
System of oppression is socially learned & reinforced	Introspection & awareness about attitudes, emotions & behaviors regarding oppression	Racial identity development & cycle of socialization	Individual introspection & self-awareness provides foundation for change agents	Build alliances & support networks within & across racial groups
Structural oppression becomes internalized as white privilege & internalized racism	Skills for meeting the challenges of racism	Cycle of liberation, race-based caucuses & fish bowl activity	Building alliances & support networks within and between identity groups.	Change racist institutional polices & practices
Separation, lack of interaction & polarization between groups	Network of allies for dismantling racism individually & institutionally	Skills development & "a day in the life of a change agent" role plays / Change teams & actions planning for next steps for institutional & community change	Experiential learning & skills practice / Ongoing personal & professional support for institutional & community change	Build inclusive organizations & communities

CHALLENGING WHITE SUPREMACY WORKSHOP

> *"White privilege is a major barrier to building the kind of social movements that could bring fundamental change to this country. Social justice activists have a real stake in tearing down this barrier."*

CHALLENGING WHITE SUPREMACY WORKSHOP

SUMMARY INFORMATION

ORGANIZATIONAL FOCUS	**Problem:** White supremacy in the U.S., structural racism, historic oppression. **Solution:** Social change and racial justice movements, anti-racist white activism, grassroots organizing leadership development.
ORGANIZATIONAL HISTORY & CONTEXT	Founded in 1993 by Sharon Martinas and Mickey Ellinger. Rooted in grassroots organizing and activism for social justice. Mission: "...to train white social justice activists to become principled and effective anti-racist organizers—both to challenge white privilege and work for racial justice in all social justice efforts."
THEORY OF PRACTICE	Anti-Racism.
ORGANIZATIONAL CAPACITY	National office in San Francisco. Ten to twelve trainers, five to six partnering organizations. Challenging White Supremacy training curriculum and reading materials.
SERVICES	Fifteen-week "Becoming an Anti-Racist Activist" workshop. Half-day workshop for global justice programs and activists.
TYPES OF PARTICIPANTS	White, grassroots, social justice activists.
LEVEL OF ANALYSIS	Structural.
PROBLEM ANALYSIS	Racism is rooted in white supremacy, a historically based, institutionally perpetuated system of exploitation and oppression that has provided power and privilege to people whose ancestors came from Europe.
INTERVENTION PRINCIPLES	Creating a mass-based, multi-racial anti-racism movement involves helping white social justice activists become principled and effective anti-racist organizers whose work can complement and support grassroots organizing and leadership in communities of color and provide anti-racist leadership in white communities.
INTERVENTION METHODS	Standard fifteen-week training model. Workshop as a learning laboratory. Presentation, small group exercises and discussion, and reflection on application as primary learning tools.
INTENDED OUTCOMES	Promote new understandings of white supremacy and structural racism. Develop an anti-racist culture of resistance. Support united, anti-racist organizing and activism. Support self-determination in Communities of Color. Create principled, grassroots anti-racist organizations and social movements. Anti-racist leadership development.
THEORY OF CHANGE	Critical analysis of political, social, and economic conditions creates new consciousness. Informal network of anti-racist leadership helps organize change. Use grassroots, anti-racist organizing strategies. Strategic collaborations with activists of color. Ongoing dialogue, action and reflection on racial justice efforts. Organize grassroots, multi-racial revolution.
CONTACT INFORMATION	Coordinators: Sharon Martinas and Chris Crass 2440 16th St., PMB #275, San Francisco, CA 94103 email: cws@igc.org

Mission & History

The Challenging White Supremacy program (CWS) was established in 1993 by Sharon Martinas and Mickey Ellinger with a mission to "...train white social justice activists to become principled and effective anti-racist organizers—both to challenge white privilege and work for racial justice in all social justice efforts." Like Crossroads Ministry, CWS's structural analysis of racism is inspired by the People's Institute for Survival and Beyond. CWS offers an important complement to these programs by focusing on training white, grassroots activists in a fifteen-week, anti-racism workshop and offering extensive anti-racism curricula and reading materials. Developed in response to the needs of experienced, white, social justice activists, the training model provides in-depth understandings of how white supremacy was created in the U.S., how it functions today, and what strategies might be useful in challenging it. The workshops serve as learning laboratories for grassroots organizers to prepare for, implement, reflect on and evaluate the anti-racist work they do in their organizations and communities.

CWS's training model has its roots in political activism for racial justice, leftist or socialist organizing, and nationalist movements of the 1960s that supported self-determination for communities of color. CWS believes that building mass-based, multi-racial, radical and revolutionary movements led by activists of color is the most powerful and effective way to bring about fundamental, revolutionary transformation of the U. S. The program focuses on examining racially oppressive ideologies that are historically based and both consciously and unconsciously reproduced in actions throughout U.S. political, economic and social systems. White social change activists who struggle

---

SETTING THE SCENE

IN A LOCAL non-profit organization in San Francisco's Mission District, the Challenging White Supremacy (CWS) program is conducting the third session of its fifteen-week workshop. Seventy-five participants, ages 20-35, sit in a large circle listening intently as the guest speaker finishes her presentation about U.S. colonialism, imperialism and indigenous resistance.

"What do you do when people have no interest in recognizing the structural dimensions of racism?" asks the presenter. Participants are silent for a moment, considering the question and thinking about their readings on this topic over the past week.

"Most of the people I work with are resistant to acknowledging, let alone giving up their privilege as whites. They don't feel privileged. They even consider themselves victims...either of poverty, sexism, homophobia, anti-Semitism or some other form of oppression...We have to explain how white supremacy is an integral part of our history, institutions and political, economic and social systems," suggests a young, white man sitting near the far corner of the room.

"And most people seem stuck talking about individual prejudices. We need better ways of giving them real information about structural racism and we need better tools for organizing," explains the young Latino woman sitting next to him.

There are murmurs of agreement around the room and the large-group discussion continues with intensity and enthusiasm for the next fifteen minutes, until the presenter calls a break. As participants get up to stretch, talk in small groups, and help themselves to the home-cooked snacks that many have brought to share, a strong sense of community and excitement pervades. The buzz of laughter and camaraderie continue throughout the break, but participants are soon eager to meet in their separate groups. The 25 white participants move off to a separate room to meet with Challenging White Supremacy workshop leaders, while the 50 participants of color remain in the larger room to meet with leaders from the partnering organization, the Institute for Multiracial Justice.

As in each of the sessions of the workshop, participants in these separate groups have a chance to explore their insights and reactions to the presentations and assigned readings, discuss the challenges and successes of their practical organizing work, and reflect on their new understandings of racism and white privilege. These discussions help develop a supportive, core group of white anti-racist organizers, build alliances across racial lines, and lay the foundations for a healthy and vibrant anti-racist movement.

for racial justice and challenge white privilege provide crucial support to leadership and organizing efforts in communities of color. In addition, the program helps develop informal networks of white anti-racist leadership in social justice organizations.

Organizational Capacity

CWS has one national office in San Francisco. The program currently offers a fifteen-week "Becoming an Anti-Racist Activist" workshop in the Bay Area where participants meet for a half-day each week to develop in-depth, practical understandings about racism in order to challenge both racial oppression and white privilege. In addition, CWS offers short, half-day "Anti-Racism for Global Justice" workshops and presentations across the U.S. that develop an anti-racist analysis of how global capitalism operates and build an informal leadership network of organizers who bring an anti-racist perspective to the movement for global justice. The program is currently developing a website to make its anti-racism curricula and other training materials available to wider audiences. CWS has 10-12 core trainers/facilitators and works with 5-6 cooperating organizations. The program's "Becoming an Anti-Racist Activist" is conducted in collaboration with the Institute for Multi-Racial Justice in San Francisco—an organization committed to combating division and building alliances among people of color.

CWS's model recognizes interrelating systems of oppression in the U.S. such as capitalism, imperialism, patriarchy and heterosexism and acknowledges individual, cultural, institutional, military and other manifestations of racism. Like the People's Institute, however, the model focuses on structural dimensions of racism and suggests that racial oppression and division has been the primary barrier to building a united, social justice movement in the U.S. CWS also focuses on the binary dynamics between whites and people of color, rather than varied relations between people of color.

Types of Participants

CWS works primarily with experienced, white, community organizers or those social activists dedicated to struggles for social justice both in the U.S. and abroad. The shorter workshops are offered to global justice activists and other participants across the U.S, while the fifteen-week training is designed for radical activist communities in California's Bay Area. The program selects participants based on their experience level with social justice activism, their political goals, and their ability to commit to the full fifteen-week training program. CWS tends to attract leaders in their 20-30s and suggests that training young, white activists in anti-racist analysis and organizing is an important and often neglected component of building a multi-cultural, anti-racism movement in the U.S.

CWS recognizes that white people and people of color have different needs in anti-racism training. The program offers important opportunities for white activists to have separate meetings. At the same time, CWS partners with the Institute for Multi-Racial Justice which offers parallel workshops for people of color. The two programs strategize and collaborate together on organizing effective anti-racism activities.

UNDERSTANDING & INTERVENING AGAINST RACISM

Understanding the Problem

CWS brings a strong historical analysis and political activism to its work against structural racism. The program traces the history of racism from European colonists' military conquest and theft of indigenous people's lands, kidnapping and enslavement of Africans to work the stolen land, exploitation of Chinese and Mexican labor, and invasion of nations of color such as Puerto Rico, Hawaii, Guam and Cuba. The program looks in detail at the web of institutional and cultural white privilege that has roots in the policies and practices of this country's "Founding Fathers" and myths of "Manifest Destiny." For example, the program looks at the "divide and control" strategies of 17th century slave owners that prevented oppressed groups from uniting by offering privileges such as land and freedom to "whites" (e.g., poor European immigrants) that were denied to people of color, and severely punishing white people who organized with Africans. These racial divisions are recreated in current social movements such as trade union organizing, environmental activism and anti-global capitalism struggles.

CWS's training model suggests that when white activists protest militantly against their own oppression while refusing to challenge racism, they become accomplices in the oppression of people of color. They also sacrifice coalitions and alliances with people of color that could effectively challenge existing oppressive power systems. CWS examines how U.S. systems of capitalism, imperialism, neo-colonialism and neo-liberalism have reinforced and recreated systems of racial oppression and white supremacy.

CWS also explores the 'campaign of confusion about racism,' or ways that language can confuse understandings of racism. The program suggests that using terms such as prejudice, discrimination, race relations, diversity and multiculturalism interchangeably with racism and anti-racism obscures distinctions between individual and systemic forms of oppression and conceals conflicting underlying assumptions about the nature of the problem. In addition, concepts such as 'reverse racism' ignore social power dynamics and comparing racism to other forms of oppression such as sexism, classism, and heterosexism, sets up false analogies that marginalize people of color, deny historical and institutional primacy of racial oppression, and create competing victimizations between groups.

Addressing the Problem

CWS's training model suggests that the best way to address these problems is to conduct anti-racist training workshops in white communities and help white social justice activists become principled and effective anti-racist organizers. The program outlines six moral and political principles for creating an anti-racist agenda. These include: 1) acting on anti-racist principles such as respect, equity, freedom and justice; 2) creating a culture of resistance to white supremacy; 3) standing in solidarity with other social justice struggles; 4) prioritizing issues of radical activists of color; 5) respecting the leadership of radical activists of color; and 6) holding on to a vision of living in an anti-racist community.

The training model also focuses on grassroots, anti-racist organizing strategies. For example, the program trains participants in the "Each One Teach One" strategy used by African Americans in the Southern U.S. in the 1950s and 1960s. Using this method, organizers engage in intensive, one-on-one communication to bring another person into the struggle for racial justice. The program also works to create core anti-racist groups where activists learn to support each other and keep each other accountable. CWS's white core groups work to build strategic alliances with activists of color. These collaborations bring multiple perspectives and establish a dialogue that strengthens anti-racist work and forms the nucleus for anti-racist transformation in organizations and communities. CWS also teaches young activists to work from a moral imperative, ensure that principles are translated into practice, and apply pressure, where needed, to changing unjust power structures.

> *" White experience becomes the unquestioned, assumed basis for examining what happens to all people. When white social justice activists use false universals and false analogies, they betray the depth of cultural racism and arrogance that plagues all white people in this country."*

CWS believes that ongoing, anti-racist education is essential for white, social justice activists, and the program trains participants to lead anti-racism education programs within their own communities and organizations. The workshops also help participants create grassroots, anti-racist organizations and develop a broad-based, anti-racist social movement.

> "The most effective way to create fundamental social change in the U.S. is mass-based, multi-racial grassroots movements led by radical activists of color... White social justice activists have a special responsibility to work for racial justice and challenge white privilege in all our social justice work."

Training Methods

CWS's fifteen-week "Becoming an Anti-Racist Activist" workshop is structured much like a university course. Participants meet for three hours a week for presentations and small group exercises and are assigned reading, journaling and practical homework between the sessions. Trainers have different political views yet model collaboration in their work together.

The structured nature of the training minimizes self-disclosure in large group discussions, but leaves room for sharing personal experiences during small-group and paired discussions. Participants receive two, large workshop binders at the beginning of the training: one consists of extensive handouts, discussion questions, exercises, articles and other training materials; the other contains both recommended and required anti-racism readings for the workshop.

The workshop begins with a full-day orientation about anti-racism work including a significant number of definitions and an analytical framework similar to that of the People's Institute. Subsequent meetings provide an overview of White Supremacy, the history of U.S. colonialism, imperialism and indigenous resistance, and a power analysis of political, economic and social systems in the U.S. Additional sessions examine capitalism and white privilege in the U.S., legacies of indigenous, black, Chicano/Latino and Asian/Pacific Island liberation. Participants are given an opportunity to look at family histories or "herstories" and review how patterns of privilege, oppression and resistance have shaped them. Finally, a number of sessions focus on tools for racial justice organizing, organizing against patriarchy and heterosexism, and building multi-racial alliances.

THEORY OF CHANGE

CWS's model holds that a critical analysis of historical and current social, political and economic relations is fundamental to building mass-based movements for social justice and change. The training model suggests that activists of color should lead grassroots, multi-racial social justice movements, however, white anti-racist activists can play both a supportive role to people of color and an important leadership role within their own communities. CWS believes that providing white activists with new understandings of how white privilege operates in the U.S. and with new skills for organizing against racism can help build solidarity across racial lines. A core group of white anti-racists can initiate a ripple effect for social change within their organizations and communities. CWS sees anti-racist work as an ongoing, revolutionary process that requires continual dialogue, action and reflection to address social power dynamics, reconcile cultural differences, and create principled social transformation.

DISTINGUISHING FEATURES

CWS is one of the few programs in the U.S. with materials and methods designed specifically for working with white social activists on issues of structural racism. The workshop's fifteen-week structure recognizes that most adults need more than a weekend training to change deep-rooted beliefs and behaviors associated with white privilege. The design provides a learning laboratory for anti-racist organizing, and opportunities for dialogue, action and reflection are integrated into the structure. In addition, the program has some of the most extensive training materials and collection of articles with a historical and structural analysis of racism available. It is also one of the few programs that combines training in anti-racism analysis with specific organizing skills and techniques for social justice work.

Finally, the program fosters an exciting and energetic sense of community among participants. The workshop's intense atmosphere creates a network of vibrant relationships essential for developing local and national anti-racist movements.

CHALLENGING WHITE SUPREMACY WORKSHOP

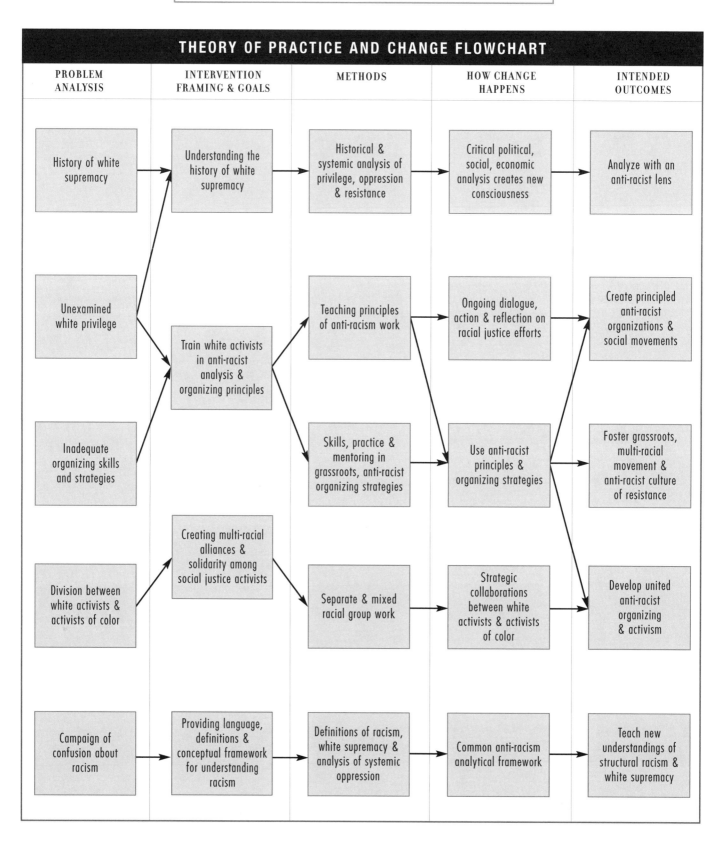

THEORY OF PRACTICE AND CHANGE FLOWCHART

PROBLEM ANALYSIS	INTERVENTION FRAMING & GOALS	METHODS	HOW CHANGE HAPPENS	INTENDED OUTCOMES
History of white supremacy	Understanding the history of white supremacy	Historical & systemic analysis of privilege, oppression & resistance	Critical political, social, economic analysis creates new consciousness	Analyze with an anti-racist lens
Unexamined white privilege	Train white activists in anti-racist analysis & organizing principles	Teaching principles of anti-racism work	Ongoing dialogue, action & reflection on racial justice efforts	Create principled anti-racist organizations & social movements
Inadequate organizing skills and strategies		Skills, practice & mentoring in grassroots, anti-racist organizing strategies	Use anti-racist principles & organizing strategies	Foster grassroots, multi-racial movement & anti-racist culture of resistance
Division between white activists & activists of color	Creating multi-racial alliances & solidarity among social justice activists	Separate & mixed racial group work	Strategic collaborations between white activists & activists of color	Develop united anti-racist organizing & activism
Campaign of confusion about racism	Providing language, definitions & conceptual framework for understanding racism	Definitions of racism, white supremacy & analysis of systemic oppression	Common anti-racism analytical framework	Teach new understandings of structural racism & white supremacy

WHITE PEOPLE WORKING
ON RACISM—TRAINING FOR CHANGE

> *"Collusion through*
>
> *silence and non-action*
>
> *is the way we keep*
>
> *the cycle of racism going.*
>
> *The greatest chasm for*
>
> *white people to cross is*
>
> *to begin taking action*
>
> *when it brings the possibility*
>
> *of breaking ranks."*

WHITE PEOPLE WORKING ON RACISM—Training For Change

SUMMARY INFORMATION

ORGANIZATIONAL FOCUS	**Problem:** Historic oppression and privilege, social ranking and marginalization, idealized self image, dichotomous thinking, white fear and judgment. **Solution:** Historic and cultural analysis of racism, self-awareness and self-acceptance, anti-racist white activism, racial justice.
ORGANIZATIONAL HISTORY & CONTEXT	Established in 1997 as a Training for Change Program. Rooted in nonviolent social activism and process psychology. Mission: "…to spread the skills of democratic, nonviolent social change and help groups stand up for justice, peace and environmental harmony."
THEORY OF PRACTICE	Anti-Racism. Prejudice Reduction and Healing and Reconciliation.
ORGANIZATIONAL CAPACITY	National office in Philadelphia. Regional office in Minneapolis/St. Paul. Three anti-racism trainers. Eight core Training for Change trainers. Three, two-day White People Working on Racism trainings (Parts I, II & III).
SERVICES	Variety of trainings on classism, nonviolent social action and training of trainers.
TYPES OF PARTICIPANTS	Broad range of white community activists.
LEVEL OF ANALYSIS	Individual, Intergroup and Structural.
PROBLEM ANALYSIS	Racism in the U.S. is historically based, individually learned and reinforced by existing social, political, legal and economic institutions and practices. Unacknowledged social rankings afford white people more power, privilege and advantage. White people's idealized self image and defenses against their fear, guilt and judgments are barriers to self-acceptance and effective anti-racism action.
INTERVENTION PRINCIPLES	To break the cycle of racism, white people must develop personal awareness; educate themselves about the history of racism in the U.S. and current manifestations at the individual, group and system levels; use their position, power and privilege to eliminate racism; build anti-racism support networks with other whites and people of color; and develop practical skills and action plans.
INTERVENTION METHODS	Part I: Building common understandings, personal awareness and skills. Part II: Developing individualized action plans. Part III: Evaluating progress. Flexible design for Part II & III based on group needs. Experiential learning, small group exercises, dialogue and simulations as primary learning tools.
INTENDED OUTCOMES	Promote understanding and awareness in whites about U.S. racism. White people as anti-racist allies and support for people of color. Empower participants as change agents. Support non-violent, anti-racist, grassroots activism.
THEORY OF CHANGE	Cognitive and emotional self-awareness and self acceptance leads to more effective action. Address barriers and form support networks. Develop skills and plan individual and grassroots, non-violent social action.
CONTACT INFORMATION	Trainers: Antje Mattheus and Lorraine Marino; Director: George Lakey 1501 Cherry St., Philadelphia, PA 19102 phone: 215-241-7035 www.TrainingForChange.org

Mission & History

Training for Change was established in 1992 by George Lakey with a mission to "...spread the skills of democratic, nonviolent social change and help groups stand up for justice, peace and environmental harmony." Recognizing the need to support white anti-racist activists, in 1997 the organization launched its three-part "White People Working on Racism" workshop. The workshop series addresses the prevalence of U.S. racism at the individual, group and systemic levels and is designed for white people who are upset by the racism around them and are searching for ways to begin or to deepen their anti-racism work. Combining cognitive, emotional and behavioral dimensions of anti-racism work, the workshop uses individual and small group experiential learning to foster personal awareness and individual action steps for addressing systemic racism.

All of Training for Change's workshops are rooted in theories and practice of non-violent social action and aligned with the values of Martin Luther King Jr. and Ghandi. Their methodology draws strongly from process psychology and integrates techniques from human relations, Gestalt psychology, Re-evaluation Counseling, Arnold Mindell and Paolo Friere.

The program focuses on empowering people to discover their own expertise and eliciting group wisdom rather than providing curriculum-centered trainings or transferring specific knowledge. Trainers suggest that the way workshops are led is just as important as the content in fostering liberation, democracy and racial justice. Training for Change programs aim to support existing social change movements

---

SETTING THE SCENE

ON A WARM Saturday afternoon in July, 10 participants in the White People Working on Racism workshop sit comfortably in a semi-circle in the Director of Training for Change's living room. Participants are silent as they write notes to themselves about their personal barriers to taking action against racism. "What are some of these barriers?" one trainer finally asks.

Participants glance down at their notes and call out some responses. "I'm too busy." "I'm not sure what to do." "I want to do it well or not at all." "I don't want to jeopardize my family or job." "I'm afraid it will take over me life." "I'm too shy and introverted." "Racism is not really a constant pressure for me, lots of times I don't even think about it." "The problems are too big, what difference can I make anyway...so why bother?"

"Our resistance has a lot of energy," comments one of the trainers. "What can we learn by looking directly at this resistance?" She looks at one of the participants, and asks, "How does it feel when you recognize that the problems are complex and big...that you can't fix racism?"

"I feel helpless," the participant explains.

"Yes," the trainer empathizes, "underneath the resistance is usually a feeling we don't want to feel. Well, lets look at this further...If the problems too big and you can't do anything, why not just do nothing?"

"But I can't do that!" the participant looks very uncomfortable for a moment and then, recognizing the 'all or nothing' thinking she has become trapped in suggests, "I guess I need to forgive myself for not being able to do everything and recognize that there are pieces I can do."

"Excellent," encourages the trainer. "We have to let ourselves express our resistance and feel those unwanted feelings. That's part of the challenge for white people working on racism—its often hard to access these feelings. But this is really the route to shifting our dichotomous, "either/or" thinking to accessing our core self and wisdom, and to feeling empowered to take action against racism."

Participants spend the next hour working in dyads on their resistance to doing anti-racism work. By the end of the workshop participants will use these new understandings to take risks in building skills and planning action against racism in their respective communities and organizations. The workshop helps them recognize that there is no recipe book for fighting racism, but a number of principles can help guide their actions and support them in their anti-racism work.

---

and help develop advanced skills for creating a racism-free world, local decision-making, empowerment for all people and environmentally friendly ways of living.

Organizational Capacity

Training for Change has 8 core trainers, 3 of whom focus on the White People Working on Racism workshops. The organization offers the White People Working on Racism series each year at its national office in Philadelphia and at it's regional office in Minneapolis/St.Paul for participants from all over the country. These trainings focus exclusively on racism in U.S. communities, however Training for Change conducts many of its other workshops internationally.

Most of the organization's other workshops focus on training methodology (rather than specific content areas) including: advanced training for social action trainers; creative workshop design; non-violence training; and facilitating transformational work, among others. The organization works specifically on integrating a variety of training methodologies and on developing programs to address important, but neglected topics for social activists. It also focuses on transferring cutting edge knowledge and techniques from the corporate sector and organizational settings to activists doing community work.

"We look at what's missing at any given time— what's not offered for activists— or what's offered in a way we don't think is effective enough. What was missing four to five years ago when we started this program was trainings for white people confronting racism."

Types of Participants

The White People Working on Racism workshops are offered to a broad audience of white people who are interested in confronting U.S. racism in their lives and work. Participants come from a variety of community settings representing their organizations or only themselves. The program especially aims to support young activists and to bring them together with more experienced activists to promote cross-generational learning and address inter-generational misunderstandings. While the workshop specifically addresses the dynamics between white people and people of color, it also acknowledges the importance of working on the diversity and conflict among communities of color.

UNDERSTANDING & INTERVENING AGAINST RACISM

Understanding the Problem

The White People Working on Racism workshops briefly trace the history of racial politics in the U.S. and review some of the practices, periods and events that formed the concept of race, racism and present-day race relations in the U.S. The model recognizes that four hundred years of oppression have created tremendous systemic disadvantages for many people of color in terms of education, wealth, health and job opportunities.

The workshop focuses on unacknowledged white privilege as a major barrier to anti-racism work. For example, trainers discuss theories of racial rank—or power that a racial group has relative to other groups—and suggests that members of higher ranking groups (i.e., white people in the U.S.) often do not recognize their rank or the privileges it affords them. Trainers highlight a variety of theories and belief systems that reinforce racial ranking and serve to blind white people to systemic forms of racism and the marginalization of other racial and cultural groups. The model suggests that when white people acknowledge racism, they often tend to intellectualize the issues and spend too much time talking about them rather than experiencing the emotional impact of racism and taking anti-racist action. Ignoring or denying emotions makes it easier for whites to lapse into unconscious collusion in perpetuating systemic racism.

Finally, the workshop looks at people's idealized self-image—or the image of how people want others to see them (e.g., wanting to be seen as the "good" or "enlightened" white)—as perpetuating the cycle of racism. The model suggests that people's idealized self-image keeps them from acknowledging their own prejudices, biases and imperfections, and prevents them from taking risks. The dichotomous thinking (e.g., things are all good, or all bad) of these defenses creates barriers to self-acceptance, undermines efforts to address the complexity of racism, and prevents racial healing.

Addressing the Problem

The White People Working on Racism training model suggests that the best way to address these problems is to provide white social activists with opportunities to develop self-awareness about being white in a racist society, and create concrete anti-racism action plans for work in their organizations and communities. The program emphasizes the importance of surfacing one's unexamined feelings and attitudes about race in order to make conscious, anti-racist choices. It also emphasizes the importance of translating new awareness into action and provides opportunities for practicing skills to do so.

The program also focuses on helping participants understand and acknowledge how white privilege, power and high rank are inherent in mainstream U.S. culture and intrinsic to white identity development. Working with fear and guilt—emotions that many white people want to avoid and that keep them from taking action—is an important part of the workshop. Trainers also assist participants in challenging their idealized self-image, acknowledging personal imperfections, and developing both

> *"Anti-racist activists can easily become judge and jury of others who seem to be the beneficiaries and perpetrators of racism. We must question our need to be "the good white" and make others "bad." This attitude only serves to make ourselves feel better by reducing others' worth and is a sure way to alienate the people we want to influence."*

humility and courage to take risks in speaking out, questioning and confronting racism without righteousness. They encourage white people to get feedback from people of color without defending or explaining themselves, and to become comfortable with conflict, chaos and strong feelings when addressing racial issues.

Finally, the White People Working on Racism program helps develop basic skills for addressing racism including effective communication, compassionate confrontation, conflict management and community building skills. Trainers stress the importance of building alliances and support networks with other white people doing anti-racism work and with people of color. These skills and networks become vital in moving toward the program's ultimate goal of advancing anti-racist social action.

Training Methods

The White People Working on Racism training is organized as a series of three weekend workshops.[9] Part I, The Persistence of Racism, is the most structured of the series, providing definitions of terms, a brief review of U.S. history of racism, theories that support racism, and basic assumptions and understandings of anti-racism work. Part I also focuses on developing participants' awareness about their attitudes and emotions connected with race. Experiential exercises ask participants to identify some of the messages they received about race growing up, to recall when they first realized that they were white, to remember a time when they were marginalized, and to describe their idealized self-image or how they would like to be seen regarding racism. The workshop focuses on practicing specific skills and behaviors to

---

9. The researchers were only able to attend the first of these three sessions and base their analysis and summary on this limited experience.

address different issues related to racism with which participants are struggling. It also provides an opportunity for participants to begin developing a personal action plan.

Part II and Part III of the series are progressively less structured and more focused on participants' specific needs for enhancing their anti-racism work. Part II, Action Planning, assists participants in designing individualized action plans for doing anti-racism work in their organization and/or community. Part III, Evaluating our Progress, helps participants assess their progress, address resistance or other issues that have emerged during their work, and plan next steps.

The White People Working on Racism workshops, like other Training for Change programs, is grounded in a number of 'core technologies.' For example, the program focuses on experiential learning and an emergent design based on the needs and wisdom of participants. Trainers recognize diversity and racism not only through the training content, but also through unwitting expressions and group dynamics during the training process. The program operates on the principal that both deep learning and social change require risk. Trainers intentionally create a container that encourages participants to take risks in the form of self-disclosure, exploration of feelings, and learning from mistakes.

Workshop participants receive a short training manual that includes explanations of core concepts, illustrations of program theories, training exercises and a useful bibliography about white identity development and anti-racism work. Trainers also provide generous handouts and articles throughout the training to supplement the presentation of information.

THEORY OF CHANGE

Training for Change suggests that individual learning and self-awareness emerge from experiencing risk, conflict and mistakes, especially if they are balanced by humor, fun and reflection. The workshop aims to help empower participants to see themselves as agents of social change and take leadership roles within their respective organizations and communities. The program suggests that anti-racism training for white people can have an important multiplier effect when participants influence their personal and professional networks and form coalitions with other anti-racist activists. Finally, the program holds that supporting grassroots, non-violent, social movements and offering advanced training for activists is the most effective means for achieving their goals of promoting local decision-making, empowering people, and creating a racism-free world.

DISTINGUISHING FEATURES

Training for Change's White People Working on Racism workshop focuses on the specific issues and needs of white people who are interested in confronting racism. The workshop provides an environment that recognizes the individual, group and systemic levels of racism and draws upon a number of social and psychological theories for understanding race relations in the U.S. The programs' dual focus on personal awareness and social action supports trainers' integration of cognitive, affective and behavioral dimensions of anti-racism work. Finally, trainers are committed to a unique methodology that emphasizes eliciting group wisdom rather than the transmitting trainer's knowledge, focuses on processes as much as content, and works with participants' risk, resistance and discomfort in order to create the deep learning needed to effect social change. The program offers a distinctive and innovative training methodology for anti-racist trainer and leadership development.

THEORY OF PRACTICE AND CHANGE FLOWCHART

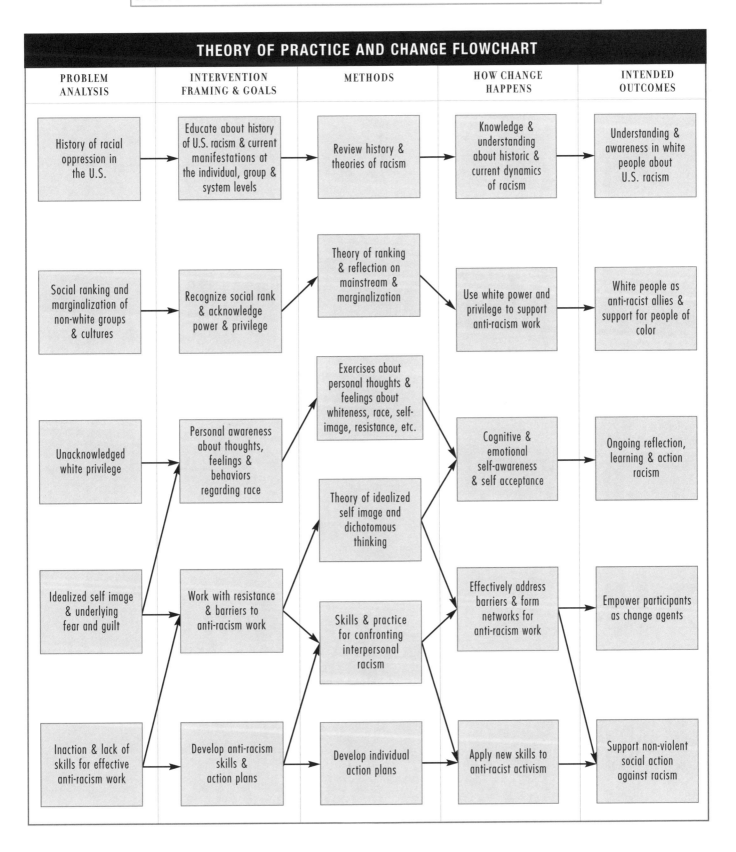

PROBLEM ANALYSIS	INTERVENTION FRAMING & GOALS	METHODS	HOW CHANGE HAPPENS	INTENDED OUTCOMES
History of racial oppression in the U.S.	Educate about history of U.S. racism & current manifestations at the individual, group & system levels	Review history & theories of racism	Knowledge & understanding about historic & current dynamics of racism	Understanding & awareness in white people about U.S. racism
Social ranking and marginalization of non-white groups & cultures	Recognize social rank & acknowledge power & privilege	Theory of ranking & reflection on mainstream & marginalization	Use white power and privilege to support anti-racism work	White people as anti-racist allies & support for people of color
Unacknowledged white privilege	Personal awareness about thoughts, feelings & behaviors regarding race	Exercises about personal thoughts & feelings about whiteness, race, self-image, resistance, etc.	Cognitive & emotional self-awareness & self acceptance	Ongoing reflection, learning & action racism
Idealized self image & underlying fear and guilt	Work with resistance & barriers to anti-racism work	Theory of idealized self image and dichotomous thinking	Effectively address barriers & form networks for anti-racism work	Empower participants as change agents
Inaction & lack of skills for effective anti-racism work	Develop anti-racism skills & action plans	Skills & practice for confronting interpersonal racism	Apply new skills to anti-racist activism	Support non-violent social action against racism
		Develop individual action plans		

SECTION TWO

IMPORTANT
RELATED WORK

SEEKING EDUCATIONAL EQUITY & DIVERSITY
[S.E.E.D.]

Established in 1987, Seeking Educational Equity and Diversity (SEED) is a *"national and international educational effort across disciplines and age levels to create school curricula, climates and teaching methods which reflect the reality that women and men of all races, classes, and ethnic groups contribute to the creation of culture and knowledge."* Co-directed by Peggy McIntosh and Emily Style, the program is based at the Wellesley College Center for Research on Women and has roots in feminist, multicultural scholarship. SEED is a voluntary network of local, teacher-led seminars in public and private schools that foster intellectual and personal faculty development. The program prepares educators to facilitate both personal and social analysis of gender, race, class and other interconnected systems of oppression and create more gender balanced, multiculturally equitable, developmentally appropriate and globally aware curricula and teaching strategies.

SEED offers year-long, monthly seminars for 10-20 teachers or other school staff from public or private schools in a given region to examine contemporary scholarship as well as the "textbooks of our lives." More than 22,000 educators in 33 U.S. states and 10 countries have participated in these school-based seminars, and many of the programs' participants have voluntarily chosen to continue meeting for years. SEED conducts three week-long summer leadership workshops for educators who wish to become seminar facilitators at their school sites. These workshops help build the network of SEED facilitators, and provide participants with opportunities to experience and discuss the emotional and intellectual dynamics of facilitating seminars on multicultural pedagogy, curricula and institutional change. Participants in SEED's summer leadership workshops must be sponsored by their educational institutions and supported in offering the monthly seminars during the subsequent academic year.

SEED seminars are circles of in-depth, on-going conversation and exploration into the ways in which members of a culture have been socialized to ignore or focus on, oppress or celebrate, engage with or cut off, the diversity of race, gender, class, sexual orientation, religion and other differences. Seminar participants explore, through a variety of different processes, how internalized, externalized, institutional and systemic forms of oppression affect all aspects of schooling. Habitual ways of seeing (and ignoring) people's life stories and oppressive cultural systems are clearly visible in the choices of teaching methods, classroom decoration, curriculum content, and interaction in school environments.

SEED's unique training model puts teachers at the center of a process for growth and development to help build their capacity for creating classrooms and schools where authentic, diverse student-centered learning is fostered. SEED holds that recognizing individuals as the authorities on their own life experiences is intimately and politically related to helping them listen to others, young and old, as the authorities on their own experiences. In addition, the program suggests that unless faculty and staff members critically reflect upon the ways they were taught (or not

"As a developmental equity project, SEED maintains that intellectual, personal and organizational development, supported over time, is essential if today's schools are to offer knowledge accurately and attend well to matters of human growth and development in the face of varied cultural realities."

taught) to deal with diversity, they cannot help students do so. SEED seminars use reflective processes, interactive exercises and discussion of articles, books, poetry and videos to help increase teachers' and students' abilities to see systemically, and recognize and respect plural dimensions in cultures not customarily studied in school curricula or reinforced in school climates.

SEED's training model posits that individual and institutional transformation is interdependent and must be supported over an extended period of time. In addition, it holds that educational materials, strategies and environments that recognize multiple forms of oppression and multiple forms of diversity are necessary for building a more inclusive, pluralistic and democratic society.

CONTACT INFORMATION:

Co-Directors: Peggy McInstosh and Emily Style
Wellesley College Center for Research on Women
Wellesley, MA 02481
Phone: (973) 763-6378 or (781) 283-2520
Fax: (973) 763-5670 or (781) 283-2504

Change*work*, was established in 1995 by Kenneth Jones, Tema Okun, Karimah Nonyameko, and Jean Gauna to *"...support social justice organizations in achieving their missions effectively."*[10] Change*work's* Dismantling Racism program uses an organizational development model designed to meet the needs of social justice organizations wanting to address issues of race and racism. The program blends both social justice organizing and organizational development theories and shares a common analysis of structural racism with the People's Institute for Survival and Beyond, Crossroads Ministry, and Challenging White Supremacy Workshop. Like each of these programs, however, Change*work* has built upon and integrated other elements into this analysis, developed a distinct application, and works with a unique methodology. The training model mentions a variety of forms of oppression, but focuses specifically on racism.

Change*work's* dismantling racism process takes place over a period of eighteen to twenty-four months and involves three distinct stages. The first stage includes an organizational assessment that examines organizations' structures, culture, relationships, issues of racism and white privilege, readiness for dismantling racism work and leaders who should participate in change teams and race-based caucuses. The second stage includes two workshops set a month or so apart. The first workshop helps build relationships and provides a common analysis for

> *"Racism is a fierce, ever-present, challenging force, one that has structured the thinking, behavior and actions of individuals and institutions since the first Europeans set foot on this continent. To understand racism and effectively begin dismantling it requires an equally fierce, consistent and committed effort."*

understanding racism as a basis for further work. The second workshop helps participants figure out where their organization is in relation to their anti-racist goals, and develops change teams and caucuses to assist in planning and implementing action steps. The third stage of the dismantling racism process includes strategic planning and visioning for long-term organizational change. This involves ongoing reflection and evaluation of the organization's progress and lessons learned over an eighteen-month period. During the workshops and consultations participants receive innovative training materials and a number of useful organizational assessment and development tools.

Change*work's* training model reviews the historic, systemic and pervasive legacies of racism in the U.S. and the process of socialization and internalization that hold the cycle of oppression in place. The program offers an analysis of racism embedded at the personal, institutional and cultural levels, identifies sources and tactics of resistance to dismantling racism, and discusses the stages and characteristics of anti-racist organizational development. The training also addresses specific dilemmas faced by change agents and provides an inventory for assessing an organization's progress in reaching anti-racist goals.

Change*work's* model suggests that anti-racist change in organizations and the communities where they work is based on a cyclical, problem-solving process involving: awareness,

---

10. Changework is not a 501 (c)(3) or other legal entity, but a collection of trainers and facilitators that specialize in anti-racism and organizational development work.

information gathering, analysis, visioning/planning, action and evaluation. The process is led and organized by change teams within organizations that are supported and informed by caucuses. Long term commitment, as well as ongoing support and evaluation, are critical to this process of anti-racist organizational and social change.

CONTACT INFORMATION:
Co-Directors: Tema Okun and Kenneth Jones
1705 Wallace Street
Durham, NC 27707
Phone: (919) 490-4448

HEALING THE HEART OF DIVERSITY

Healing the Heart of Diversity (HHD) was established in 1997 to *"...foster social change, develop effective ways to collaborate, resolve differences and build productive work teams."* Through the program, people who do diversity work in corporations, non-profit organizations, educational institutions and communities experience renewal, changes in the "habits of the mind," and a sense of healing. The program is based on research and change theory in transpersonal and cognitive psychology, emotional intelligence and transformative learning.

HHD offers national "train the trainers" programs that provide diversity professionals and social change leaders with an opportunity for personal reflection and transformation that can renew their spirit and passion for diversity work. The program consists of a series of three or four intensive retreats, totaling more than one hundred-twenty hours over a one-year period. Offered in four locations—Washington, D.C., California, Virginia and Michigan—this training helps participants gain mastery in the HHD change process. HHD also designs customized programs and retreats in communities upon request.

HHD aims to increase participants' capacities to lead and sustain change, strengthen decision-making, manage relationships, communicate effectively and interact with an extensive learning community. The program helps participants access individual and collective wisdom and deepen their knowledge of themselves and others. Participants also learn how to apply their newly acquired skills to advance the impact of other, on-going leadership and diversity programs in their communities and workplaces.

Cultural transformation can become a reality when those who "do their own work" apply their personal HHD transformational experience in their outer lives and work.

The program utilizes processes such as critical reflection, dialogue, inquiry, collaborative learning and networking and supports participants in developing deeper understandings of important diversity issues such as racism, sexism, heterosexism, cultural myths and discrimination in the workplace and community. The program integrates contemplative and spiritual practice, as well as emotional and reflective dimensions of diversity work to facilitate constructive action and help participants enhance their capacity and competence in leading cultural and institutional change. HHD suggests that personal consciousness, healing, and collaboration with others provides a basis for effective professional actions beyond the retreat setting.

HHD takes a participant-centered approach and creates a safe, learning community that provides opportunities for addressing specific diversity issues, working through personal and group concerns and sharing authentically with others of diverse backgrounds, experiences and perspectives. Participants rigorously engage in another dimension of leadership—"leading from within"—and work with the most pervasive social issues of our time to explore the possibility of a breakthrough to a new paradigm where living and working together is a celebration of common humanity.

The program's theory of change suggests that authentic change is a conscious choice resulting from individual awareness and experience. When individuals make a commitment to inner change, they can take action outwardly. Authentic interaction in a diverse community leads to deeper understanding of oneself and others, and can contribute to social healing. Systemic change can occur in organizations, communities and institutions when aligned with individual and personal change.

CONTACT INFORMATION:
Director: Patricia Harbour,
712 Staunton Ave, N.W.
Roanoke, VA 24016-1036
Phone: (540) 343-5192
hthd@mindspring.com
www.healingtheheart.org

THE NATIONAL NETWORK OF ANTI-RACISM & COMMUNITY BUILDING TRAINING INSTITUTES

The National Network of Anti-Racism and Community Building Training Institutes (National Network) was developed in early 2000 to *"… increase the quantity and quality of civic leadership dedicated to advancing anti-racism work at the local and regional levels."* This joint anti-racism venture between the Institute for Democratic Renewal at Claremont Graduate University and Project Change, an anti-racism initiative founded by the Levi Strauss Foundation, combines several separate anti-racism components into a single seven-day training institute. These anti-racism training institutes integrate a structural analysis of racism with community organizing skills and approaches, and apply them to different areas of institutional racism (e.g., education, public health, police/community relations, and regional economic development). Designed to provide participants with a comprehensive base of knowledge, skills and practical applications, the institutes coordinate and bring together a number of anti-racism organizations and professionals who have different but complimentary areas of expertise.

The National Network currently offers the training institutes several times a year at each of its four regional sites including: Albuquerque, NM; Seattle, WA; Broward County, FL and New Orleans, LA. Each training institute averages approximately 25 participants representing a wide spectrum of individuals and organizations engaged in a variety of community building and anti-racism efforts.

> *We are responding to the questions that people on the ground repeatedly ask at the conclusion of most short, single-element trainings: "Where do we go from here? How do we relate our new 'theoretical' understanding to the real live situation in which we are living? Although we know a growing amount about a number of discreet things, how do we integrate our knowledge into a coherent, informed action plan?"*

The National Network's training model brings together a number of separate organizations in a collaborative effort to offer a core curriculum that is adapted to focus on issues in particular neighborhoods, organizations or topic areas. Each of the seven-day trainings begins with the People's Institute's intensive two-day undoing racism training. Building on this analytical framework of structural racism, a former director of the Center for Third World Organizing has made available a curriculum for anti-racism community organizing skills and information, customized to address specific regional and participant needs. During the last two-three days of a training, a host of local organizations and professionals at each site work with participants to apply the anti-racism analysis and skills to specific topic areas such as healthcare, education, judicial/legal, fair lending and economic development.

The National Network's training model aims to create long-term, structural change by building the capacity of community leaders to sharpen their understanding of institutional racism and collectively organize, plan and implement specific anti-racist actions within their own communities. The model suggests that by flexibly linking and coordinating a variety of existing anti-racism organizations and professionals, participants can be provided a combination of analysis, skills and applications that is more comprehensive than its component parts. The collaboration of different anti-racism trainers and work with diverse participants also fosters long-term local, regional and national networks to advance community building and social change efforts toward racial justice in a revitalized democracy.

CONTACT INFORMATION:
John D. Maguire
Institute for Democratic Renewal
Claremont Graduate University
Claremont, CA 91711-6163
Phone: (909) 607-9220
Fax: (909) 607-9221
john.maguire@cgu.edu

Shirley Strong
Project Change
678 13th Street
Oakland, CA 94612
Phone: (510) 663-0148
Fax: (510) 663-0153
sstrong@projectchange.org

SECTION THREE

People's Institute for Survival and Beyond • National Coalition Building Institute • VISIONS—Vigorous InterventionS into Ongoing Natural Settings • World of Difference Institute—Anti-Defamation League • Crossroads Ministry • Study Circles Resource Center • Hope in the Cities • Dismantling Racism Institute • National Conference for Community and Justice • Challenging White Supremacy Workshop • White People Working on Racism—Training for Change • People's

SIMILARITIES & DIFFERENCES ACROSS PROGRAMS

SIMILARITIES & DIFFERENCES
ACROSS PROGRAMS

The summaries in Sections One describe the nuances found within each training program. This section analyzes and compares some core elements across programs, as a tool for further reflection. Like the summaries, the comparison examines programs' contexts, analysis of problems and framing of interventions, training methods and theories of change. Rather than comparing each program point by point, the discussion focuses on the larger themes related to theories of practice and change.

PROGRAM CONTEXTS

All of the programs we studied labor in a difficult environment: They address the complex, deep-rooted, shifting dynamics of racism, racial and ethnic conflict and intergroup relations in fast-paced and constantly changing environments. They do groundbreaking work in addressing these difficult issues with relatively few financial resources and limited time commitments from participants. Programs meet these challenges in the following ways.

Programs emphasize the dynamic nature of their practice. Program directors and trainers suggest that their knowledge and practice continually evolves, responds and adapts to a variety of external and internal factors. For instance, influential factors outside the programs include changing demographics and intergroup relationships, national and community events, participant needs and funding opportunities. Factors within the programs include trial-and-error learning, trainers' expertise and experience, and the programs' mission and vision.

Contextual factors—such as program size, duration, philosophical roots, funding sources, budgets, staff development, and trainer diversity and expertise—also shape how programs respond to the dynamic environment in which they work. They impact programs' selection of services, breadth of reach, and ability to respond to new demands. They also influence how and in which communities a program develops trust, recognition and credibility. And they certainly affect programs' efforts to attract and maintain adequate financial and human resources.

Programs work with a variety of participants, tailoring the training process to different groups' needs. Most programs work with multiracial groups of participants, bringing together people from diverse backgrounds, experiences and perspectives to learn from each other. These mixed groups provide important opportunities for participants to deepen understanding, build empathy and develop cooperative relationships and networks across racial lines.

All of the programs we reviewed also recognize that populations have specific training needs and, increasingly, trainers are developing separate, race-based programs. For example, National Coalition Building Institute (NCBI) and the Dismantling Racism Institute (DR) both have race-based caucuses that define their own training agendas and help shape work in multiracial groups. The People's Institute, Challenging White Supremacy Workshop (CWS) and Training for Change have designed content and methods specifically for

> *A Prejudice Reduction trainer might say, "the world is filled with wounded people who are doing the best they can with the resources they have available to them. Once people understand their own oppression and are tied into a healthy network, they can act as agents of change."*

work with people of color (People's Institute) or white people (CWS and Training for Change). These separate meetings provide a unique environment for deeper exploration of group-specific issues and leadership development.

> *An anti-racism trainer might say,*
> *"The world is controlled by powerful systems*
> *with historically traceable roots.*
> *Once people are shown how they benefit*
> *from or are battered by those systems,*
> *they can work together to change the systems."*

Participant selection processes vary widely across programs, driven by the program's theory of change. Some welcome all individuals; others select people to represent a cross-section of the community; and some recruit participants with specific professional backgrounds, leadership levels or types of experience.

ANALYSIS OF PROBLEMS & APPROACHES TO TRAINING

The way in which a program names and frames the problem it addresses constitutes a theory of practice. Among these selected training programs, words such as "prejudice," "racism," "intolerance" and "racial conflict" have strong and often subtle meanings that are not consistent from group to group. Because language is a window into a deeper worldview of how people see problems and solutions, we examined the key words used by these training programs to identify and delineate their approaches to problem-solving. The broad range of language and frameworks we found suggests that many theories of practice are in play.

The Theories of Practice chart shows some of the variation in programs' theories of practice organized into categories described by program trainers and materials.[11] Our comparison, which shares characteristics with previous analysis (e.g., Delgado, 1992;

> *A Healing and Reconciliation trainer might say,*
> *"the world is filled with groups that have been*
> *traumatized and victimized by historic events.*
> *When the oppressing group acknowledges and*
> *apologizes for these injustices,*
> *individual and social healing, reconciliation,*
> *and transformation can occur."*

Shearer, 1992), and also forges some new ground, provides a conceptual map for understanding the current landscape of trainings addressing racial and ethnic oppression. Still, it cannot capture the richness, complexity and uniqueness of any one program.

The chart highlights differences, rather than similarities, and does not show relationships between types of programs. Yet many of the theories of practice overlap in complementary ways. Programs that frame problems and interventions in more than one way thus appear in more than one category (e.g., VISIONS, DR Institute, Training for Change).

Our review of theories of practice revealed several notable differences in approaches. Although the differences often reflect tensions, we think they can be viewed as complementary, rather than competing, viewpoints. Some of the major distinctions among programs are outlined below.

Emphasis placed on culture and power. Programs that focus on eliminating racism emphasize power issues when discussing the sources of racial inequity, injustice and conflict. Programs that focus on diversity and multicultural approaches, on the other hand, emphasize ignorance or bias about cultural differences when discussing the sources of racial, ethnic and cultural miscommunication, misunderstanding and conflict. While these are quite different analysis of the core problem, the frameworks often overlap in discussions of cultural oppression, privilege or monoculturalism.

---

11. This typology and the following Levels of Analysis chart emerged from the comparative analysis of programs in this study and additional overlapping research (Shapiro, I., 2002).

THEORIES OF PRACTICE

	PREJUDICE REDUCTION	HEALING & RECONCILIATION	ANTI-RACISM	DIVERSITY/ MULTICULTURALISM	DEMOCRACY BUILDING
KEY WORDS	Prejudice, stereotypes, past wounds, healing, emotion work.	Historic traumas & injustices, acknowledgment, forgiveness, healing.	Racial oppression, white privilege, power, social justice.	Mono/multi-culturalism, diversity, inclusion, tolerance.	Citizen participation, civic infrastructure, deliberative processes.
PROBLEM ANALYSIS	People engage in oppressive acts or hurt others because they have been oppressed or hurt.	Traditions of division & inequity have traumatized & victimized certain groups. Lack of acknowledgement & forgiveness hold destructive patterns of interaction in place.	Current social, economic, & political systems give power & privilege to whites & deny the same to people of color. Lack of a common analysis of structural racism is a barrier to building a united social justice movement.	People do not have information or awareness of other cultures & have few skills for interacting with them. People devalue contributions of other groups or cultures.	People are separated and disenfranchised. They lack forums, processes & skills for effectively addressing the growing diversity & complexity of racism & race relations.
INTERVENTION FRAMING	Become aware of own oppression & address emotions. Build alliances with others across barriers of race, ethnicity & culture.	Allow groups to share their stories & histories. Encourage acknowledgement, repentance & forgiveness of injustices.	Provide analytical framework for examining systemic forces at work in the community (cultural, economic, institutional, political, etc.).	Develop critical perspective about social messages & biases. Promote understanding & appreciation of other cultures.	Construct deliberative, public forums & processes to promote inclusive, engaged, cooperation of citizens across non-profit, business & govn't sectors.
WORLD VIEW*	"The world is filled with wounded people who are doing the best they can with the resources they have available to them. Once people understand their own oppression & are tied into a healthy network, they can act as agents of change."	"The world is filled with groups that have been traumatized & victimized by historic events. When the oppressing group acknowledges & apologizes for these injustices, individual & social healing, reconciliation & transformation can occur."	"The world is controlled by powerful systems with historically traceable roots. Once people are shown how they benefit from or are battered by those systems, they can work together to change the systems."	"The world is filled with a multitude of complex cultures, constantly intersecting & shaping each other. As people grow to understand & appreciate their own culture & cultures around them, they will be better able to cooperate & overcome mutual problems."	"The world is filled with diverse perspectives on complex issues such as race. When people have appropriate public forums, processes & skills for dialoguing about these issues, they will recognize their interdependence & find cooperative ways to address common concerns."
THEORETICAL TRADITIONS	Psychology & Psychoanalytic theory; Re-evaluation Counseling.	Multi-faith spiritual & religious traditions; Group Psychoanalytic theory.	Sociology; History; Liberation Theory.	Cultural Studies; Social Psychology; Management.	Political Science, Social Capital; Deep Democracy.
INTENDED OUTCOMES	Personal awareness & healing; skills for addressing prejudice; alliances within & across groups.	Individual transformation; dialogue between groups; transformed relationships; public healing & reconciliation.	Social change toward equity & justice; self-determination; empowerment for activism.	Awareness of cultural differences; tolerance, inclusion & respect of other cultures; improved intergroup relations.	Engaged citizenry; participation toward common understandings; collaborative decision-making; new civic infrastructure.
TRAINING PROGRAMS	- National Coalition Building Institute - VISIONS - Training for Change - Dismantling Racism Institute (NCCJ)	- Hope in the Cities - Training for Change	- People's Institute for Survival & Beyond - Challenging White Supremacy Workshop - Crossroads Ministry - Dismantling Racism Institute (NCCJ) - VISIONS-Training for Change	- World of Difference Institute (ADL) - Dismantling Racism Institute (NCCJ) - VISIONS	- Study Circles Resource Center

* World View quotes for Prejudice Reduction, Anti-Racism, and Diversity/Multicultural theories of practice are taken from, Shearer, J.M. (Spring, 1992) "Race Relations: Three Paradigms." *Conciliation Quarterly,* 11(2), pp. 4-6.

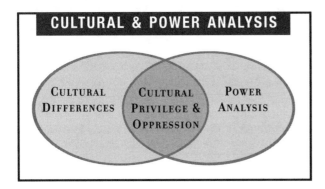

Goals of training. The theories of practice used by training programs promote a variety of goals including racial healing, reconciliation, tolerance and justice that correspond to deep spiritual, psychological, social and political dimensions of race relations work. For example:

- Programs oriented toward "Prejudice Reduction" often include the emotional and psychological dimensions of racial healing.

- Programs whose theory of practice seeks "Healing and Reconciliation" often focus on social and spiritual dimensions of racial healing, reconciliation and peace.

- Programs that focus on "Diversity and Multiculturalism" or "Democracy Building" often address social, cultural and political issues of racial inclusion and tolerance.

- Programs with "Anti-Racism" goals often emphasize social, political and economic issues of racial justice and equity.

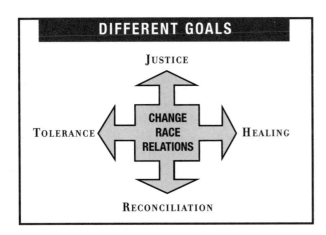

While a program's approach generally emphasizes just one goal, the categories are not exclusive. It is reasonable to think of the goals as interdependent, emanating from the same need for social change but driving practice in somewhat different directions.

A focus on differences and common ground among racial, ethnic and cultural groups. Programs that emphasize "Prejudice Reduction" and "Healing and Reconciliation" practices tend to focus on how similar people really are. For them, change stems from developing empathy, recognizing a shared humanity, and revealing common ground. In contrast, programs whose theory of practice involves "Anti-Racism," "Diversity and Multiculturalism" and "Democracy Building" focus on understanding and appreciating differences among racial, ethnic and cultural groups. For them, change becomes possible when people acknowledge and respect diverse experiences, views, needs, histories and cultures.

These distinctions play out in the policy environment in controversies over strategies to address similarities and differences, such as "colorblind" or "affirmative action" programs. Still, many people agree that constructive change must include *both* a recognition of differences and some agreement on common ground.

Level of analysis: individuals, intergroup relationships, or structures and institutions. Most programs work on all of these levels to some degree, but they usually favor one level as the starting point for understanding problems and initiating change. The chart below illustrates some differences between levels of analysis.

Training programs that work primarily with individuals are by far the most prevalent. Even organizations whose activities address several levels of change tend to focus their practical training efforts on individuals. This approach may be popular for several reasons. First, a focus on individuals is aligned with dominant cultural values of individualism and autonomy. Second, an emphasis on personal experience and growth may make the trainings particularly relevant and appealing to people. Third, training may be a particularly effective method for promoting individual education and introspection, while other processes may be better for building relationships and advancing structural and institutional change.

Training programs that focus on intergroup relations are also numerous, for many of the same reasons. This level of analysis seeks

> *A diversity trainer might say,*
> *"The world is filled with a multitude of complex cultures, constantly intersecting and shaping each other.*
> *As people grow to understand and appreciate their own culture and cultures around them, they will be better able to cooperate and overcome mutual problems."*

to bridge individual and structural interventions by providing transformed individuals with opportunities to build resilient relationships and networks of alliances that can foster structural change. However, many scholars and practitioners seem to agree that these efforts have been more successful at developing new knowledge and expertise on intergroup processes than in mediating controversies between individual-level and systems-level approaches.

Fewer training programs in the U.S. offer a structural or systemic analysis of racism. Such analysis challenge dominant institutions and

LEVELS OF ANALYSIS CHART

	INDIVIDUAL	INTERGROUP	STRUCTURAL
FOCUS OF ANALYSIS	Individual attitudes, assumptions, identities, feelings & behaviors.	Racial, ethnic and cultural group relations.	Systemic oppression in institutions, policies & practices.
ISSUES	Prejudice, bias, stereotype, bigotry, internalized oppression/privilege, resistance & defenses, feelings of anger, guilt, fear, individual racism.	In-groups/out-groups, group separation & polarization, community conflict, diversity, leadership, ethnocentrism, cultural racism.	Racial privilege/oppression, racial disparity, stratification, disenfranchisement, injustice, institutional & structural racism.
THEORY & RESEARCH TRADITIONS	Psychology, Counseling.	Social Psychology, Cultural Studies.	Sociology, History, Political Theory, Macro-economics.
THEORIES OF CHANGE	*Individual Change:* Introspection & education. *Social Change:* Individual influence within personal & professional spheres; critical mass of transformed individuals.	*Intergroup Change:* Small group contact; sharing personal stories & experiences. *Social Change:* Respectful, trusting relationships; cooperative networks, alliances & coalitions.	*Social Change:* Community organizing, activism and advocacy; common analytic framework for change; united social movements; institutional & policy change.
INTENDED OUTCOMES	Personal awareness & healing; new interpersonal skills & behaviors; individual cognitive, emotional & behavioral transformation.	Appreciate differences; recognize common ground; improved communication; cooperative planning and problem-solving; accountable leadership; participation; inclusion.	Accountable institutions; self-determination in communities of color; equity; justice; access and opportunity; integrated communities.

© Shapiro, Ilana. (2002). *Mapping Theories of Practice and Change: A Comparative Analysis of Programs Addressing Racial and Ethnic Tensions in U.S. Communities.* George Mason University. Doctoral Dissertation.

cultural myths of meritocracy in ways that resonate strongly within many communities of color. They also draw attention to the subtle and often coded forms of institutional oppression that characterize modern racism, and they confront the status quo by recognizing power imbalances in race relations.

> *A democracy building trainer might say, "The world is filled with diverse perspectives on complex issues such as race. When people have appropriate public forums, processes and skills for dialoguing about these issues, they will recognize their interdependence and find cooperative ways to address common concerns."*

Recognizing of the effects of oppression. All of the training programs reviewed in this *Guide* recognize the interdependence of various forms of oppression (e.g., racism, classism, sexism, heterosexism, ageism) and the cumulative effect that multiple forms of oppression can have. The programs also try to respect the struggles of all oppressed groups and discourage competition over who is most victimized. But programs differ considerably in whether they focus on the unique history and manifestations of racism or examine dynamics across several forms of oppression.

For example, NCBI, World of Difference® Institute and VISIONS emphasize the similar dynamics and impacts of various forms of oppression in an attempt to build empathy across groups, overcome resistance to acknowledging racism, and create an inclusive anti-oppression movement. In contrast, programs offered by the People's Institute, CWS, Crossroads Ministry, DR Institute, Hope in the Cities, Training for Change and Study Circles focus specifically on racism. They view it as a powerful, enduring and defining legacy in U.S. communities and institutions that often is unacknowledged or subsumed by a focus on gender, poverty or other social issues.

Emotional dimensions of the work. All of the training programs acknowledge the cognitive, affective and behavioral dimensions of building racial equity and inclusion. However, most curricula emphasize cognitive and behavioral changes, such as new insights, analysis, awareness

and skills. When participants express strong feelings, trainers must rely on their own skills rather than programmatic strategies to manage the group's emotions and refocus participants. Only a few of the programs we reviewed, such as NCBI and Visions, integrate conceptual and practical tools for working with participants' feelings into the training design.

TRAINING METHODS

The design, format, tools and materials used for training varied across programs in the following ways:

Training design. As venues for practical education, training programs usually are much more structured and directive than technical assistance, dialogue, visioning, cooperative planning and problem-solving programs and other methods. Nevertheless, the programs included in this *Guide* varied considerably in the flexibility of their training design.

At one end of the continuum, programs such as People's Institute and NCBI have very structured models. Trainers vary their emphasis and examples but, in general, the programs focus on core understandings of racism, oppression, and prejudice that are consistent across groups and situations. At the other end of the continuum, programs such as Training for Change and World of Difference® Institute follow some key design principles but frequently adapt and reconfigure their models to address the needs of specific groups and situations.

Programs also differ in how prescriptive or elicitive they are with participants. Prescriptive models, such as CWS, provide basic information and common understandings about racism that help everyone "get on the same page." These are largely curriculum-centered models

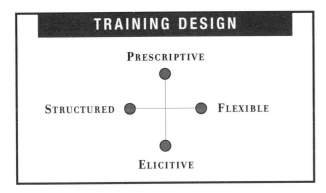

TRAINING DESIGN

PRESCRIPTIVE

STRUCTURED — FLEXIBLE

ELICITIVE

that share trainer expertise and help participants integrate new knowledge into their own contexts. Models such as Training for Change, Study Circles and Hope in the Cities, take a more elicitive approach that "start where participants are" and build from their understanding of issues. These participant-centered approaches empower people to draw from their own expertise and discover new knowledge.

Training format. Most organizations recognize the need for sustained, multifaceted efforts to address racial and ethnic oppression. Practical experience, however, suggests that short, discrete trainings are most accessible and attractive to participants. Programs have developed a number of strategies for addressing this difficulty. Most identify their short trainings as a first step in a longer process of building racial equity and inclusion. Programs such as CWS, Training for Change, Crossroads Ministry, DR Institute and Study Circles offer longer programs with multiple components and try to gain participant commitment from the beginning. This ensures that participants get a deeper, more sophisticated understanding of issues and supports them in applying their new learning within their organizations, institutions and communities.

NCBI, People's Institute, World of Difference®, Visions and Hope in the Cities take a somewhat different approach, offering technical assistance and customized programs as follow up to an initial short training. This offers participants an important foundation for deeper work and allows flexibility in deciding the most appropriate next steps.

Learning tools. All of the programs in this *Guide* incorporate adult learning principles and address varied learning styles within their training design. For example, they provide a clear structure for new concepts and information, offer interactive activities that engage participants in learning, and work with multiple senses through videos, presentation, small and large group discussions, role playing, cultural rituals and other methods. The DR Institute and World of Difference® Institute, in particular, use many diverse, innovative exercises. In addition, World of Difference® Institute, Study Circles, Hope in the Cities and Training for Change encourage participants to discover new ideas and lessons themselves.

Almost all of the training programs help participants communicate effectively and interact respectfully. While several programs use similar exercises to address topics such as internalized oppression and the history of racism in the U.S., trainers usually draw out unique lessons with participants.

Materials. Programs vary in the types of materials they provide to participants. These include:

- Large binders with a wealth of articles, bibliographies, charts of key concepts, worksheets for exercises, and other resources that supplement information covered during the training (Crossroads Ministry, DR Institute, Challenging White Supremacy).

- Abbreviated manuals or handouts designed for a particular group, targeting concepts and exercises directly relevant to the training program (VISIONS, Training for Change, People's Institute, Hope in the Cities).

- Polished manuals or guides that describe the relationships between program philosophy and specific learning tools and exercises (Study Circles, World of Difference® Institute, NCBI).

THEORIES OF CHANGE

Myriad forces shape programs' theories of change, but three factors stand out as especially strong influences: the participants served, theories of practice and levels of analysis. These factors combine uniquely in each program to suggest who should lead change, what should be changed (and why), and where change should begin. For example:

- Some suggest that transformed individuals will lead structural change, and build more equitable and inclusive institutions. Others suggest that inclusive, equitable structures will lead to the transformation of individuals who live and work in them.

- Some programs create an environment that makes participants feel safe for taking risks; others challenge participants to step outside their comfort zone.

- Some train participants to end the criticism and oppression of people who try to organize, promote and lead community change. Others train new kinds of leaders who are more accountable to the communities they serve.

Despite these differences in philosophies and methods, the programs are united around many core values: empowerment, responsibility, empathy, respect, equity, inclusiveness and humanism. In addition, although they recognize how slow and frustrating the change process can be, they share an optimism about people's ability to learn, change and transform society. The programs all aim to motivate and cultivate personal, relational and structural change, and they encourage participants to be leaders and change agents in their communities and organizations.

The programs also share many ideas about how change happens. For example, most believe that participants need more self-awareness, knowledge about racial oppression, and skills and strategies for combating racism. Most programs view strong leadership and strategic coalitions as important ingredients for change. And, by focusing on training, they embrace grassroots (bottom-up) and relationship-building (middle-out) strategies, rather than top-down approaches to social change.

This brief analysis can only highlight some of the broad themes that emerge from a review of training programs. The categories and distinctions outlined here are sketches; they cannot capture the subtleties of individual programs, and they should not be used to confine or delimit a program, or fuel debate over approaches. Rather, this discussion aims to stimulate further reflection about the evolution of these models for building inclusive and equitable communities. A major part of that discussion, addressed in the final section of this *Guide*, involves the struggles and opportunities that these programs face.

SECTION FOUR

People's Institute for Survival and Beyond • National Coalition Building Institute • VISIONS—Vigorous InterventionS into Ongoing Natural Settings • World of Difference Institute—Anti-Defamation League • Crossroads Ministry • Study Circles Resource Center • Hope in the Cities • Dismantling Racism Institute—National Conference for Community and Justice • Challenging White Supremacy Workshop • White People Working on Racism—Training for Change • People's Seed—Seeking Educational Equity and Diversity • Changework • Crossroads Ministry • Study Circles Resource Center • Healing the Heart of Diversity • Hope in the Cities • National Network of Anti-Racism and Community Building Institutes • Dismantling Racism Institute-National Conference for Community and Justice • National Coalition Building Institute • People's Institute for Survival and Beyond • National Coalition Building Institute

CHALLENGES & IMPLICATIONS

The comparison of programs in Section Three outlines some of the unresolved questions, conflicts and challenges in efforts to build racial equity and inclusion. These tensions, which often surface as critiques of particular training programs or approaches, actually reflect much larger public debates that are also played out in policy and research arenas. This section discusses some of those tensions, highlights the relevant lessons drawn from our program review, and suggests implications for future training efforts.

Three overarching, interrelated themes emerged from our study, and they shape the discussion that follows:

1. We must strengthen training efforts to understand and combat structural racism. Programs draw from a healthy variety of psychological and cultural theories and use well-developed methods to address prejudice, bias, internalized oppression, diversity and intergroup relations. Those efforts provide important opportunities to stimulate personal growth and healing, and improve relationships among people from diverse backgrounds, experiences and perspectives. But too few efforts are grounded in sociological, political and economic theories that directly address the structural dimensions of racism—and too few programs transcend individual and intergroup relations to address systemic racism. We need to support, develop and integrate more sophisticated analysis and practical tools for understanding and changing the web of institutional policies, practices and power structures that shape American communities.

2. We must advance efforts to translate awareness into action. Training programs currently use an excellent array of methods to foster personal reflection, insight and awareness. They impart information, build awareness, and facilitate understanding of issues—effects that can transform participants and prepare them to generate social change. But understanding the problems of racial and ethnic oppression does not necessarily solve them. Training programs need more explicit and specific strategies for helping people apply what they learn within their organizations, institutions and communities. We must support efforts to develop innovative tools, skills and practical resources that translate personal awareness into real solutions.

3. We must encourage coordinated and sustained change efforts. Trainers work in demanding and competitive environments, and they rarely have opportunities to cooperate and learn from each other. If we hope to dismantle racism, however, we will need to draw upon a variety of theories of practice and change and build on promising practices across programs. We also will need to enhance the effects of training by pairing it with other intervention methods such as cooperative planning and problem-solving, community organizing, and community building. Fostering cooperation and coordination among approaches and methods can help build upon existing successes, and offer more sustained activities to interrupt the dynamics of racism that divide and damage U.S. communities.

CHALLENGES

The goals embedded in the above themes are achievable, but not easily. Judging from the experiences of programs in this *Guide*, the key challenges are to: clarify language, differentiate among types of oppression, address the emotional aspects of racism, expand time and financial commitments, evaluate progress, and extend the reach of training.

Clarifying language. Race and racism are notoriously difficult to talk about in the U.S. Conversations often are politically and emotionally charged, fraught with dissenting opinions and experiences, and mired in complex, interrelated issues. The many terms used to describe groups (e.g., "race," "ethnicity," "cultural," "minority"), issues (e.g., "prejudice," "oppression," "racism," "intolerance," "race relations") and approaches (e.g., "prejudice reduction," "anti-racism," "healing and reconciliation," "diversity management," "multiculturalism") are laden with unspoken assumptions. They allow people to talk past each other without really communicating. It is not necessary to reach consensus, but it is essential to understand the nuances of our language if we seek productive conversations and unified action on racial issues.

Differentiating types of oppression. Most training programs—even those designed explicitly to address racial and ethnic oppression—focus on aspects of oppression that play out similarly for various populations. This practice fosters empathy and support among oppressed people—an essential ingredient for personal and social change. But a focus on similarities misses important distinctions about the sources and dynamics that shape oppression. It also risks suggesting that oppressed groups are interchangeable. Further, it discounts the unique histories and conditions that have shaped racism in the U.S. and the variety of experiences among racialized groups. For example, the prejudice and oppression directed at some commercially successful Asian Americans appears to have more in common with expressions of anti-Semitism than with the type of racism facing African Americans.

Addressing the emotional aspects of racism. All programs in this *Guide* seem to recognize that strong emotions are an integral part of the struggle against racial oppression. But it is a considerable challenge to work with participants' emotions in ways that integrate the personal and political dimensions of racism. Even programs that directly address participants' emotions must improve efforts to ensure that trainers create safe space, allow sufficient time, and develop adequate skills to help participants work positively with the feelings that surface.

Expanding time and financial commitments. Participants' and funders' limited time and financial commitments significantly shape programs. Funders usually concentrate their resources on specific "projects" or "products" and are reluctant to support ongoing efforts. In addition, participants are constrained by limited time and financial resources. They generally find short-term, discrete trainings most accessible and appealing. These limited commitments create difficulties for training programs that try to make long-term change. Both funders and participants need to recognize the deep-rooted, multi-dimensional nature of this work and develop more enduring and sustained commitments.

Evaluating progress. Evaluations help programs gauge effectiveness, reflect on practices, and make in-course corrections. Most programs described in the *Guide* make some effort to evaluate the training process, participant satisfaction and any cognitive or behavioral changes produced in participants. However, few programs have a rigorous and systematic process for linking theories to outcomes or for analyzing results, which leaves them largely reliant on staff's intuition to identify and make improvements.

More work is needed to help trainers articulate their program models, rigorously assess progress toward goals, extract lessons from experiences, and apply the findings to ongoing activities. That won't be easy. Results, especially for preventive and proactive programs, often are intangible and incremental—and it's hard to attribute effects to training programs when so many other contextual factors also influence changes. At a minimum, however, programs should clearly identify desired outcomes and find more accurate ways to measure progress.

Extending the reach of training. The training programs in this *Guide* impart knowledge about prejudice, diversity and racism that build a strong and necessary foundation for further reflection, dialogue and action. But the short, discrete training sessions offered by most programs are not sufficient to produce lasting change in institutions and structures. That will require a broader, sustained plan for change across individuals, groups and systems. Many training programs are beginning to address these problems by expanding their scope and treatment of issues. More work is needed, however, to help participants implement, assess and redesign their strategies for addressing racial and ethnic oppression.

FUTURE DIRECTIONS FOR RACE-RELATED TRAINING PROGRAMS

The information contained in this *Guide* holds several implications for the design, implementation and support of race-related training programs. The following list summarizes new directions, culled from the previous sections of this *Guide*, that are especially relevant for community leaders, program staff and funders:

1. PROGRAM COORDINATION

Program directors should build alliances with other race-related initiatives and coordinate goals and methods across programs to produce a deeper understanding of racial oppression and a more diverse set of teachable skills. For example, the National Network of Anti-Racism and Community Building Training Institute (see Section Three) has begun to bring together several training efforts in a more intensive, comprehensive anti-racism initiative. By providing opportunities for programs to initiate and shape these strategic alliances and collaborative activities themselves, coordination can transcend the limits of the individual components.

Researchers should identify under which conditions each training model works best. These efforts should begin to identify criteria that help match training approaches to specific audiences, issues and situations. Funders, community leaders and organizations that have worked with several training programs can offer case studies that illustrate the different contributions that each approach can make to a specific environment.

Community and organizational leaders should integrate promising practices from a variety of race-related training approaches into existing community organizing, community building, and organizational development efforts. These programs can provide complementary analysis and skills to those efforts and ensure a focus on important racial dynamics.

2. PROGRAM DEVELOPERS

Program developers should create specialized services for specific populations. For instance, several programs have designed services for specific professional groups, such as police officers, educators and managers. These efforts can be expanded to address racial identity development and levels of experience with race-related issues.

Advanced training should include skills and methods for addressing various levels of conflict. For instance, trainers can provide analytical tools and intervention designs for situations in which tensions are escalating, have erupted in violence, or are stuck in post-crisis animosity.

Funders and program directors should focus on an expanded audience of racial, ethnic and cultural groups. In particular, programs should move beyond a binary view of race relations—such as black versus white, or whites versus people of color—to a more complex treatment of relations among racial identity groups.

Training activities should balance culture—or group-specific services—with a broader analysis of the oppression and resistance that all racialized groups experience.

3. PROGRAM EVALUATION

Program directors and funders should systematically engage researchers and evaluators to measure progress and identify the criteria for success that are appropriate for various program models.

Researchers should take up the challenge of comparative program evaluation and identify criteria for success that are appropriate across different approaches. These assessments should combine trainers' own criteria for successful interventions with those in the research literature and develop a broader conceptual framework for comparison.

Researchers must temper their search for general principles of intervention with a recognition that there are no simple recipes for addressing racial oppression and conflict across contexts.

4. MOVING FROM LESSONS TO ACTION

Trainers need more explicit strategies for helping people apply new skills and understanding within their organizations, institutions and communities. Funders should support efforts to develop innovative tools, skills and practical resources that help translate personal awareness into action.

Programs must agree on a broader vision that fosters united social action. For example, the Network of Alliances for Bridging Race and Ethnicity (NABRE) at the Joint Center for Political and Economic Studies has recognized the importance of building a common vision and united social movement for equitable and inclusive communities. Such efforts must address the practical and ideological challenges of appreciating programs' diverse theories of practice and change while identifying common ground for joint action.

Racial justice movements must build a relationship with other social movements, especially those related to poverty, human rights, globalization and the environment.

We hope this *Guide* provides some of the information stakeholders need to respond to these implications, and to engage and support training programs that address racial and ethnic diversity, oppression and conflict. In addition, we hope this *Guide* will contribute to advancing understandings of current training approaches and help ground further efforts to build more inclusive, equitable and democratic communities.

QUESTIONS GUIDING THE SELECTION OF A TRAINING PROGRAM

THESE QUESTIONS MAY BE USEFUL in selecting a training program that is appropriate to your personal, organizational or community needs.

Training Philosophy and Goals

1. What is the program's underlying philosophy regarding the significance of race in our society?
2. On what problems or issues does the training focus?
3. How does the training help change individuals, intergroup relations, and/or community structures?
4. What are the goals of the training?

Program Capacity

1. What is the program's history and roots?
2. How large is the program? (How many offices? How many trainers/staff?)
3. What types of training and other services does it offer?
4. Does the program have a specialized focus or expertise in particular issues, geographic areas or racial/ethnic/cultural groups?
5. Can the program offer multilingual training?

Participants

1. Who are the program's typical participants?
2. What is the usual group size?
3. Can they provide a client list?

Trainers

1. Who are the trainers?
2. What are their backgrounds and training experience?
3. How does the program train or prepare its trainers?

Methods and Materials

1. What training tools does the program use? (e.g., presentation, discussion, interactive exercises, role-plays, and videos)
2. What is the general structure of the training?
3. Can they provide a sample agenda?
4. What materials does the training provide to participants? What other materials are available?

Assessment

1. How does the program assess the needs of their participants?
2. How will they tailor the program to meet participants' needs?
3. How does the program evaluate its own training methods and effectiveness?
4. What has the program learned from past evaluations?
5. Can they provide references for their work?

Outcomes

1. What new skills, information, understandings, etc., will participants take away with them from the training?
2. How will participants transfer what they learned in the training to their organizations or communities?

Follow-Up and Support

1. What follow up support can the program provide after the training?
2. What is 'required' of participants after the training is over?

Commitment and Logistics

1. What time commitments are needed for the training?
2. What are the costs associated with the training?
3. Where are trainings held?
4. How often are trainings offered?

CHECKLIST
MARKS OF A HEALTHY RACE-RELATED TRAINING PROGRAM

DOES THE TRAINING PROGRAM:

- Clearly explain its theory of practice and change?
- Demonstrate consistency between what it says it does and what it actually does?
- Integrate a structural analysis of racism into its social change efforts?
- Address the different needs of diverse racial, ethnic and cultural groups in both its content and methods?
- Discuss differences among various kinds of racism and explain the relationship between racism and other forms of oppression?
- Recognize and support the variety of spiritual/moral, emotional, political, cultural and social aspects of anti-racism work?
- Help participants translate new awareness and understandings into action?
- Establish clear goals and systematically assess its contribution to changing individuals, intergroup relationships and community structures?
- Provide follow-up or support to participants beyond the training program?
- Cooperate or coordinate its activities with those of other programs working toward racial equity and inclusion?

APPENDICES

INTERVIEW QUESTIONS

A. Framing the Problem

1) What kinds of racial/ethnic problems or issues do you address in your trainings?
2) What do you consider the primary causes or sources of such problems or issues?

B. Principles and Methods for Training

1) What people, theories, or schools of thought have influenced the philosophy and methodology of this organization and training program?
2) What specific training content and methods are used in your program? Why?
3) Do you vary your trainings according to the situation or participants? If so, what influences your choice of content and your process design decisions?
4) Why do you think that your approach will be helpful in reducing intergroup tensions, oppression, or racism?

C. Expected Training Outcomes

1) In general, what are you trying to achieve with participants in the training? What are you trying to achieve beyond the trainings in communities and social relations?
2) What changes do you hope your trainings will foster in individuals? Inter-group relations? Social structures and policies?
3) What effects do you hope to see in the short-term? In the long-term?
4) What do you see as the unique advantages of the work your organization does?
5) What are the limitations?

D. Organizational Capacities

1) What types of training programs do you offer?
2) Who are the target participants for these programs?
3) Do you have specialized focus or expertise in particular issues, geographic areas, or identity groups?
4) What is the history and size of your organization?

Interviews were conducted as informal conversations with 2 or 3 trainers and staff per organization. Questions and topic areas were covered in different order and with different phrasing, depending on the natural flow of conversation.

OBSERVATIONAL PROTOCOL

TRAINING ORGANIZATION

TRAINER'S NAME(S)

OBSERVER'S NAME(S)

DATE OF TRAINING

LOCATION

WHO ARE THE PARTICIPANTS?
(How many of each?)

AGE	___ Under 21	___ 21-30 years	___ 31-40 years	___ 41-50 years	___ 51 and up
GENDER BREAKDOWN	___ Female	___ Male			

ETHNIC HERITAGE	___ African ___ Asian/Pacific Islander ___ European ___ Latino/Hispanic ___ Native American ___ Other (specify)	Use space for comments:
APPROXIMATE ANNUAL INCOME	___ ≤ $20, 000 ___ $20,000—$40, 000 ___ $40,000—$70,000 ___ $70,000—$100,000 ___ $100,000 +	Use space for comments:

EMPLOYMENT	___ Academia/Education ___ Business-Corporate ___ Law ___ Medical/Dental	___ Sciences/Engineering ___ Non-profit ___ Social Service/Justice ___ Military	___ Svc. Industry ___ Athletics ___ Arts/Entertain. ___ Other
GEOGRAPHIC INFO.	___ Local	___ Visitors	___ Other (please specify)

WHO ARE THE TRAINERS? (How many of each?)					

AGE	____ Under 21	____ 21-30 years	____ 31-40 years	____ 41-50 years	____ 51 and up
GENDER BREAKDOWN	____ Female	____ Male			

ETHNIC HERITAGE	____ African ____ Asian/Pacific Islander ____ European ____ Latino/Hispanic ____ Native American ____ Other (specify)	Use space for comments:
APPROXIMATE ANNUAL INCOME	____ ≤ $20, 000 ____ $20,000—$40, 000 ____ $40,000—$70,000 ____ $70,000—$100,000 ____ $100,000 +	Use space for comments:

EMPLOYMENT	____ Academia/Education	____ Sciences/Engineering	____ Svc. Industry
	____ Business-Corporate	____ Non-profit	____ Athletics
	____ Law	____ Social Service/Justice	____ Arts/Entertain.
	____ Medical/Dental	____ Military	____ Other

GEOGRAPHIC INFO.	____ Local	____ Visitors	____ Other (please specify)
HOW MANY OF EACH?	____ Participants	____ Trainers	

WHAT IS THE SELECTION PROCESS?

WHO IS TARGET AUDIENCE AND WHY?

HOW LONG IS THE TRAINING? IS IT RESIDENTIAL?

OBSERVATIONAL PROTOCOL

WHERE IS THE TRAINING HELD? WHAT IS THE TYPE OF FACILITY?

HOW TYPICAL IS THE TRAINING PROGRAM TO THE ORGANIZATION?

GOALS AND EXPECTATIONS

WHAT ARE THE STATED GOALS AND EXPECTATIONS OF THE TRAINERS?

HOW DO THESE COMPARE WITH THE ORGANIZATIONAL LITERATURE?

WHAT, IF ANY, ARE TRAINERS' ADDITIONAL IMPLICIT GOALS AND EXPECTATIONS?

DO PARTICIPANTS HAVE A CHANCE TO VOICE THEIR EXPECTATIONS?

IF SO, HOW DO THESE FIT WITH TRAINER'S GOALS AND EXPECTATIONS?

CAUSAL ASSUMPTIONS/EXPLANATIONS

HOW DO TRAINERS IDENTIFY "THE PROBLEM"—WHAT KIND OF LANGUAGE DO THEY USE?

HOW DO TRAINERS EXPLAIN THE CAUSES OF "THE PROBLEM"?

DOES TRAINING FOCUS ONLY ON RACISM OR ON MANY KINDS OF OPPRESSION?

IS THERE A HIERARCHY?

HOW ARE THEY CATEGORIZED? (E.G. BINARY: WHITE/PEOPLE OF COLOR; MULTI-FACETED DISTINCTIONS AMONG GROUPS, GENERATIONS, ETC.)

WHAT DISTINCTIONS ARE MADE BETWEEN PAST AND CURRENT FORMS OF OPPRESSION?

WHAT PHRASES, METAPHORS, AND SPECIFIC LANGUAGE IS USED TO ANALYZE "THE PROBLEM"?

PRINCIPLES AND METHODS

WHAT TRAINING PRINCIPLES DO THE TRAINERS ARTICULATE?

HOW IS "SAFE SPACE" ESTABLISHED?

PRINCIPLES AND METHODS

WHAT IS THE STRUCTURE AND FLOW OF TRAINING ACTIVITIES?

HOW ARE EXERCISES SETUP AND DEBRIEFED?

HOW IS THE TRAINING FORMAT VARIED? (E.G., LECTURE, SMALL GROUP EXERCISES, CASE STUDIES, VIDEOS, DISCUSSION, ETC.)

HOW ARE DIFFERENT LEARNING STYLES ADDRESSED? (E.G., SEEING, HEARING, DOING)

IS THE DEGREE OF SELF-DISCLOSURE, DIRECT CONFRONTATION, EXPRESSED EMOTION, ETC., SENSITIVE TO DIFFERENT STYLES OR COMFORT LEVELS?

HOW MUCH FOCUS IS ON: ANALYSIS OF PROBLEM? STRATEGIES/METHODS FOR ACTION? RELATIONSHIP BUILDING AMONG PARTICIPANTS? OTHER?

IS TRAINING CONSISTENT BETWEEN GROUPS? OR IS IT DEVELOPED OR ADAPTED TO MEET THE SPECIFIC NEEDS OF PARTICIPANTS?

ARE THERE DIFFERENCES IN CULTURAL STYLE RELATIVE TO WAYS OF KNOWING (EXPERIENTIAL VERSUS STORYTELLING)?

CONTENT AND EXAMPLES

WHAT ARE THE MAIN CONTENT AREAS DISCUSSED DURING THE TRAINING?

WHAT EXAMPLES DO THE TRAINERS USE TO ILLUSTRATE THEIR POINTS?

WHAT KINDS OF ISSUES OR SPECIFIC CONFLICTS ARE BEING ADDRESSED?

LEVEL OF ANALYSIS

WHAT IS THE PRIMARY LEVEL OF ANALYSIS USED BY TRAINERS: INDIVIDUAL, INTERGROUP, INSTITUTIONS, POLICY?

IS THE APPROACH PRIMARILY SOCIOLOGICAL, ANTHROPOLOGICAL, PSYCHOLOGICAL, RELIGIOUS/SPIRITUAL, OTHER? IF THERE IS AN INTEGRATED MODEL, WHAT DOES IT LOOK LIKE?

HOW DO TRAINERS SUGGEST THAT SOCIAL CHANGE HAPPENS?

WHAT IS THE PROGRAM'S VISION FOR A BETTER FUTURE?

EVALUATION

WHAT FORMS OF EVALUATION DO TRAINERS PICK UP ON AND USE?

WHAT ARE THE TRAINERS' CRITERIA FOR SUCCESS OR FAILURE OF THE TRAINING?

WHAT ARE THE EXPRESSED REACTIONS OF PARTICIPANTS?

METAPHORS

WHAT METAPHORS DO TRAINERS USE TO DESCRIBE THEIR WORK AGAINST OPPRESSION?

WHAT METAPHORS DOES THE GROUP USE?

BIBLIOGRAPHY

This list of books and articles is compiled from the bibliographies of training programs in this study and consists of those resources that were mentioned as important by at least two (and often more) training programs.

Allport, G. (1954). *The nature of prejudice.* Reading, MA: Addison-Wesley.

Barndt, J. (1990). *Dismantling racism: The continuing challenge to white America.* Philadelphia, PA: Augsberg Press.

Batts, V. (1998, May). *Modern racism: New melody for the same old tunes.* EDS Occasional Papers. Episcopal Divinity School.

Bell, D. (1992). *Faces at the bottom of the well: The permanence of racism in America.* New York: Basic Books.

Bennet, M. (1986). A developmental approach to training and intercultural sensitivity. *International Journal of Intercultural Relations,* 10. 179-196.

Bennett, L. (1993). *Before the Mayflower: A history of black America.* New York: Penguin Books.

Chisom, R. & Washington, M. (1997). *Undoing racism: A philosophy of international social change.* New Orleans: The People's Institute Press.

Corcoran, R. (2001). *Connecting communities.* Initiatives of Change.

Cross, E., Katz, J., Miller, F., & Seashore, E. (1994). *The promise of diversity.* Irwin Professional Publishing.

Dalton, H. (1995). *Racial healing: Confronting the fear between blacks and whites.* New York: Anchor Books.

Delgado, R. (Ed.). (2000). *Critical race theory: The cutting edge.* Philadelphia: Temple University Press.

DuBois, W.E.B. (1990). *The souls of black folk.* New York: Vintage Books.

Feagin, J. (2000). *Racist America: Roots, current realities and future reparations.* New York: Routledge.

Freire, P. (1972). *Pedagogy of the oppressed.* New York: Seabury Press.

Hacker, A. (1992). *Two nations: Black and white, separate, hostile, unequal.* New York: Scribner's.

Hooks, B. (1995). *Killing rage: Ending racism.* New York: Owl Books.

Katz, J. (1978). *White awareness: Handbook for anti-racism training.* Norman: University of Oklahoma Press.

Kivel, P. (1996). *Uprooting racism.* Philadelphia: New Society Publishers.

Kretzmann, J. & McKnight. (1993). *Building communities from the inside out: A path toward finding and mobilizing a community's assets.* Chicago: ACTA Publications.

Kochman, T. (1981). *Black and white styles in conflict.* Chicago: University of Chicago Press.

Loewen, J. (1995). *Lies my teacher told me: Everything your American history textbook got wrong.* New York: Simon & Schuster.

McIntosh, P. (1989, July/August). White privilege: Unpacking the invisible knapsack. *Peace and Freedom Magazine.*

Omi, M. & Winant, H. (1994). *Racial formation in the United States: From the 1960s to the 1990s,* (2nd ed.). New York: Routledge.

Ponterotto, J. & Pederson, P. (1993). *Preventing prejudice: A guide for counselors and educators.* Newbury Park: Sage Publications.

Rothenberg, P. (Ed.) (1988). *Racism and sexism, an integrated study.* St. Martin's Press.

Shearer, J. M. (1992). Race relations: Three paradigms. *Conciliation Quarterly Newsletter, 11 (2).* 4-6.

Schoene, L. & DuPraw, M. (1994). *Facing racial and cultural conflict: Tools for rebuilding community.* (2nd ed.). Washington, D.C.: Program for Community Problem Solving.

Study Circles Resource Center (1997). *Toward a more perfect union in an age of diversity: A guide for building stronger communities through public dialogue.* Pomfret, CT: Study Circles Resource Center

Takaki, R. (1993). *A different mirror: A history of multicultural America.* Boston: Little, Brown & Co.

Takaki, R. (Ed.). (1994). *From different shores: Perspectives on race and ethnicity in America,* (2nd ed.). New York: Oxford University Press.

Tatum, B.D. (1997). *"Why are all the black kids sitting together in the cafeteria?" and other conversations about race.* New York: Basic Books.

West, C. (1993). *Race matters.* Boston: Beacon Press.

Zinn, H. (1980). *A people's history of the United States: 1492-present.* New York: Harper.

Promising Practices Directories and Resource Guides on Race Relations:

Center for Living Democracy. (1997). *Interracial dialogue groups across America: A directory.* Hadley, MA: Center For Living Democracy.

Delgado, G. (1992, September). *Anti-racist work: An examination and assessment of organizational activity.* Oakland, CA: Project Change.

National Conference on Community and Justice. (1998). *Intergroup relations in the United States: Seven promising practices.* New York: National Conference for Community and Justice.

National Conference on Community and Justice. (1999). *Intergroup relations in the United States: Programs and organizations.* New York: National Conference for Community and Justice.

President's Initiative on Race. (January, 1999). *Pathways to one America in the 21st century: Promising practices for racial reconciliation.* Washington, D.C.: Government Printing Office.

Project Change. (2000). *Anti-racism resource guide.* Oakland, CA: Project Change.

Schoene, L. & DuPraw, M. (1994). *Facing racial and cultural conflict: Tools for rebuilding community.* (2nd ed.). Washington, D.C.: Program for Community Problem Solving.